Predict Through Handwriting

A leading authority offers you the key to success in love, friendship, and your career

AF528026

SYED JAFAR MAHMUD

BOOKS FOR ALL

[A Division of D.K. Publishers Distributors (P) Ltd.]

Delhi-110052

Sales Office:
D.K. PUBLISHERS DISTRIBUTORS (P) LTD.
1, Ansari Road, Darya Ganj, New Delhi-110002
Phones: 3261465, 3278368
Fax: (011) 3264368

© 1992 Publisher
Second Edition 1995

ISBN 81-7386-124-2

Published by: **BOOKS FOR ALL**
[A Division of D.K. Publishers Distributors (P) Ltd.]
at Regd. Off.: A-6, Nimri Community Centre,
Ashok Vihar, Phase-IV, Near Bharat Nagar, Delhi-110052.

Typeset by: **ABC for DTP,** Delhi-110034

Printed at:
Santosh Offset, Delhi-110035

PRINTED IN INDIA

You Can Analyze Handwriting

Handwriting can answer many personal questions about anyone. In graphology a slip of the pen is as revealing as a slip of the tounge, and when you know it, to look for even hidden character traits are as easy to read as ABC.

Now, for your own delight and knowledge, Syed Jafar Mahmud offers you quick and easy access to the unlimited secrets of your handwriting, shows you how to use graphology in public and private life, and assures you a fascinating new way to evaluate yourself and those you care about.

What A Knowledge Of Handwriting Can Do For You

Do you really know yourself? Did you know that Handwriting Mirrors Character? Would you like to learn How to See People As they Really Are?

A Knowledge of what your handwriting means, may change your life

Every time you write your name you are registering a pen picture of your personality. If you could set down your signatures in a continuous line, from your first schoolboyish scrible to that stylized autograph of yours, you would have a portrait in writing of your character from childhood to adulthood.

The story of the development of your character from year to year would be seen in the script, just as a slice of a log reveals in its concentric rings how the weather helped or retarded the growth of the tree.

But you are not felled timber. You are very much alive and growing. You have many chances to adjust your mental and physical environment so that you will grow straight and develop normally.

Handwriting reveals your present and past growth

Your handwriting will reveal the nature of your present and past growth. If it satisfies you, the next step is to study the writing of others so you may understand what is happening in their lives.

If you are not satisfied, you will want to see yourself the way your handwriting mirrors you so that you will have a true picture of your personality.

Know yourself first - then know others - then enjoy the thrill of fitting in with the whole human family because you will be in a position to understand people.

You will never again have that feeling of being alone

When you start reading characters from handwriting (the science of graphology), you will discover that many people fall into general personality types, of which you might possibly be one. You will also find out that, regardless of financial or social success, even the leaders in the community and the nation have their weaknesses. You will have revealed to yourself also, what traits of character helped them to achieve success.

You will discard that cheerless untruth that there is no one else in the world like you. You will find out that there is no one quite like you, but you have millions of general counterparts everywhere in the world.

If amazingly your handwriting evidence proves you a genius, just remember the genius is a type, too. We have had them before and expect to keep having them.

You are what you write—but you don't have to stay that way

When you look at your handwriting and classify yourself as a particular type of personality or as a complex bundle of entangled human nature you do not have to stay the way you see yourself. This book will reveal how you can change for the better and make life stimulating.

Why your handwriting reveals the real you

You are not what you think you are, not are you what other people imagine you to be. You tend to forget your faults, and you magnify your good points. Six different people will see you in six different ways.

Your handwriting will record an accurate picture of the real you because it is the end result of your brain in action, when you write, you think. To prove this, try to write an intelligent statement without keeping your mind on what you are writing. You will find it will be impossible. Your brain must tell your hand just how to write the words that you "see" in your mind. Your nervous system acts as the "wires" along which the messages of how to write travels. Hence, stimulated by the brain, your muscular system is coordinated into a more or less controlled writing movement.

Children write like children. Adults write like adults

When you were a child you wrote like a child. Your handwriting was large and slowly formed, it was awkward and lacked rhythm, and it reflected the immaturity and simplicity of your childhood.

But when you grew up you put away childish things. You wrote like the complex person into which you had matured. Your writing was no longer simple. It mirrored the character traits and the personality twists which you had acquired. The simple ingredients of childhood had become the infinitely complex blend of millions of experience which are now compositely recognized as you. And you write accordingly.

No two persons write the same way

That is why no two persons write exactly in the same way. They could not, even if they wanted to. Our whole system of credit would collapse if one person's signature were not singularly different from that of another.

The nearer you are to your early childhood, the more your writing will resemble that of a child's. The farther you have advanced maturity, or in establishing yourself as an individual, the more your script will reveal how grown up you are.

A bright new world can be yours

This book will show you how to use handwriting study to pick out personality and character clues and then how to apply many of the findings of modern psychology to help open up a bright, new world for you, for your family, for friends, and for many other people who might interest you.

Graphology will be easy for you if you add this new information to what you already know about people. The behaviour of those in your immediate family and that of close friends is bound to be fairly clear to you. Build upon this knowledge, using handwriting analysis as the master key to unlock personality mysteries.

Psychographology is the layman's answer to personality problems

In these pages you will find out about the new and highly useful science called Psychographology, which adds modern psychographological principles to the science of Graphology. You can actually "do-it-yourself" by merely looking at your own and other's handwriting.

Handwriting is your raw material. This book is your power tool

Using this book as a tool, you can work with as much handwriting as you wish to work on, and employing a full set of psychological "attachments" you will be able to understand people who have puzzled you for years, as well as find out all about yourself. This method of objective self-inspection will remove any blind spots you may have in your personality since you will not be able to reasonably dispute the scientific findings covered in the section on Graphology. You will admit any weakness in your character and will want to do something about them.

You will also learn your strengths and can build upon them for more satisfaction and profit.

Know yourself by using handwriting clues

Before you can improve your character, refine your personality, smooth your relations with others, advance in your job or succeed in business, attain happiness in marriage, get rid of unhealthy practices or attitudes, or free yourself from silly or sickening fears and frustrations, you must get a clear, personal picture. You must know yourself.

That is the first step, and handwriting analysis will make that initial pace positive and reassuring. Self-knowledge will give you confidence that you know what you are doing and that what you are doing is right. You will respect yourself for what excellent talents you will undoubtedly discover. Other people will catch the contagion of glowing self-esteem and reflect it in your direction. The doors to many situations will begin to open almost before you touch the knobs.

May be you are an engineer who secretly loves to sing, but fear of making a fool of yourself and prevented you from joining a choral group. When you find out from looking at your handwriting that you have a wonderful sense of rhythm and musical sensitivity, your fear will vanish and you will add a new happiness to your life.

Perhaps you are a banker who would be advanced into a public relations vice-presidency but you lack ability in talking before groups. A glance at your writing discloses that you have excellent spatial relation knowledge, that you have word fluency, that you have a sparkling sense of humour—but that you also have inordinate personal pride. The latter prevented you from taking a course in public speaking at the local Adult Education centre. Now that you know what held you back, that you were just blind to an important personal improvement because you thought it was beneath your dignity to "go back to school", you will drop the deadweight and advance unhampered.

You can also soft-pedal that which you cannot prevent in your personality, you can concentrate on constructive elements of your character, you can relate your interests and your vocational aptitudes to your present job and your future job advancement, you can use your new knowledge gleaned from handwriting study to solve every possible personal problem so that the solution fits the real you, as you now will now yourself.

Handwriting knowledge will show you how to get along with other people

Why is it that you find it difficult to adjust to certain persons? Is it because you can't get along with people in general? Or is it because nobody can get along with these people? Wouldn't it be helpful to know for certain which fact is true? Think of the peace of mind that would be your's if you found out that it was the other person's fault that your human relations were snarled and unpleasent. Then imagine how good you would feel if you could help that other individual to unsnarl his tangled-up character. It would be highly worthwhile if that other person were your wife, a business associate, a neighbourhood child or your own child, a fellow-worker, or the new member of the Board of Directors who came into your group via the purchase of a big block of common stock.

There are many places in life where you must get along with people. You have no other choice. Handwriting will solve this perennial problem.

Graphology is something you can study anywhere in the world at any hour of the day. Wherever there is writing or whenever you observe people penning a piece of script you will be able to discover new information about human beings. What study or science could be easier.

You won't learn everything overnight, but you won't need to. After only a few trials you will be amazed at what you will be able to tell from a mere glance at a specimen of handwriting. Each new analysis will increase your skill.

Fitting into the right job is made easier through handwriting analysis

All sorts of special talents and aptitudes are quickly seen in handwriting. Musical ability, scientific bent, dramatic feelings, mathematical skill, constructive and designing talent, artistic learnings, a natural selling sense, leadership traits, aptitude for research, a genius for working with others, promotion and merchantising senses are only a few of the job suggesters that show in handwriting.

You have only to look at your handwriting to see if you are in the right job. The right job will be the one that coincides with your interests and aptitudes. It may not be the one that pays you the most money. It will be the position that leaves you in general state of happiness rather than depressing you daily by its deadening drudgery.

Since it is only natural to be dissatisfied and to aim constantly for self-improvement, do not make the easy mistake of thinking you are a vocational misfit simply because you are not getting the most out of your life work. You may be marking time, looking for something better when you have the best chance for success and happiness in your present position. Study your handwriting to see if you are using hidden talents. May be a shift to another department in the same organization would result in doubling your salary.

Marriage happiness can be helped by using handwriting

Whether you are in the process of picking a marriage partner or whether you are already married, you will find it revealing to know more about the other person. Single individuals can avoid the shock of marrying an abnormal person. They can also select a partner with whom they would be compatible. Ideas can be matched, preferences can be considered, and physical characteristics can be checked in advance. What a man wants in a wife and what a girl desires in a husband are all plainly pictured in handwriting. You can minimize the chance of your marriage ending up in divorce if you take a little care in thinking over the characteristics displayed in your proposed partner's handwriting before you make the final decision.

Family peace can be possible by calming down the aggressors

If your household is in constant turmoil and upset due to the clashes and conflicts of different personalities, don't think that this tenseness has to continue. A study of the handwriting of the various members of your family may reveal that one or more people in the group are over-aggressive, extra-antagonistic, or supersensitive in their attitudes. Talking thing over in "family council" type of group therapy may easily eliminate much unnecessary bickering, baiting, and downright negation.

Knowledge is power, and power can spell peace. Everybody wants to be peaceful, but they must first learn how.

You will be able to understand children by examining their writing

If you are a parent or a teacher, you can use handwriting analysis to help understand children. Whether or not you help them with your new knowledge, you will get along with them better. Children know when you understand them and will cooperate more readily.

As a parent you will be interested in watching the physical, mental, and emotional progress of your child so that you can step in at the proper moments to provide the guidance and direction that only you as a parent can give. School work, friends of the opposite sex, possible vocational choices, and many other parent—child problems can be diagnosed and solved if a close study of the young person's handwriting is made.

A teacher can use handwriting knowledge to distinguish between the lazy student and the retarded learner, to note important changes in adolescent growth which would have to be considered in teaching that particular child, to spot the real juvenile delinquent, to "understand" some of the "foolish" things that school age children do, and to note the bright pupils early so that assignments might be geared to fit their precocious talent.

Businessmen can improve business relations and human relation

If you are in business you will be interested immediately in how to detect an honest worker. The handwriting of prospective employees will reveal their reliability. Business are notoriously poor judges of character; if may be because they see so many people at close range that they get confused. Everybody looks like everybody else.

Public relations is another concern of the businessman. If he fails in this important activity, his business fails along with it. A study of your handwriting may convince you that, if you do not have the proper promotional kind of personality, it might pay you to step into the background and have some other person take care of meeting the public.

If you are the "boss" and several hundred people depend upon your "mood" for their working happiness, you could decide to stabilize your personality and thus bring equanimity where before there was uncertainity. Then, too, you may have a "depresser" in your organization who makes your moodiness seem all the worse. You might get rid of him. As "boss" you have access to everybody's handwriting. It would pay you to take a look "behind the scenes".

Handwriting will warn you of unhealthy practices and attitudes

We all have our own ideas about what is good for us and what will harm us. May be we don't believe that working too hard and too fast hurts us. We may smoke, drink, overeat, lose sleep, indulge in physical excesses, and the like because we don't think other people can tell us how they harm us personally. But your handwriting will mirror you just as you are at the moment you write. It is almost like going to a doctor and having him hand you a chart giving the graphic story of your health.

If you will look at your handwriting you will see if your way of life is affecting your mental or physical health. Dissipation will show, deterioration will reveal itself, change will be immediately apparent, fear will drag itself through your writing, frustration will grip your script, and the approach of a nervous breakdown will be noted so that you can stop it before it happens.

One unsocial attitude, a single negative tangent in your living, or just too much insistence may block you from great personal success and happiness. You will believe it if you, yourself, observe it in your writing and you will undoubtedly desire to do something about changing the particular phase of your personality that is wrong.

Take this book as a hand tool, if you must, and chisel away your rough spots.

Free yourself from harmful fears through handwriting knowledge

Everybody is afraid of something, but nobody should be afraid of everything. Some people are always in a state of anxiety or worry. Your handwriting will tell you just how fearful you are, what situations cause you fright, whether the fears are temporary or permanent, and if you use the psychographological suggestions contained in this book, you will be able to erase the fears that make you miserable.

After all, how can you be afraid of something that you know all about and understand?

Stand in the dark in a strange room. Let your imagination run riot. If something touched you lightly on the top of the head, something that you did not expect, and then there was the sudden crashing of broken glass, you might possibly stand unperturbed! You also might not. Then if the lights went on and you heard the voice of someone you knew saying: "Oh, the wind must have blown the loose pane out of that window and broken it," and you looked up and noted a swinging light cord above your head, you would lose all your unfounded fears!

How certainly people can profit from handwriting revelations

A salesman can avoid irritating a prospective customer by knowing ahead of time that person's dislike.

A banker can keep his bank clear of dishonest people except bank robbers.

A probation officer can receive indication of just how far he will be able to trust his charges.

A judge will be able to corroborate his wise judgements of the truth of witness's testimony.

A lawyer will be able to size up new clients who come to him for legal advice.

A purchasing agent will be able to know just how much of a salesman's story to believe.

A social worker will be able to get closer to his people because he will be able to see behind cold facts of statistics.

A personnel manager will save himself years of useless interviewing by quick general employee screening through handwriting study.

A politician will be able to know who his real friends are.

A principal will be able to pick the best possible teachers for his school.

A Board of Education can weed out undesirables in the whole school personnel set-up.

A supervisor could select employees likely to succeed as foreman.

A chain store organization could pick their managers according to a desired chain store manager pattern.

A TV manufacturer could select people who would be able to handle detailed assembly work of TV sets.

A department store could save time and money by not hiring clerks who could not be taught to get along with customers.

A credit service could limit credit to business persons who showed too many speculative tendencies.

A wealthy person hiring domestic could know quickly the type of individuals he was employing.

A college registrar could select the "best" when the qualifications of prospective students seemed practically equal, thus assuring the "cream of the crop" for his college.

GRAPHOLOGY AT A GLANCE

The following list gives you a speedy over all view of just what handwriting analysis covers. Select the item on the right that interests you and then turn to the section on graphology to get the details.

Add what you have learned about modern psychology to this foundation material of handwriting analysis and you will be able to find out about yourself and others immediately. Read the entire book if you need refresher course in applied psychology.

The basic facts of graphology can be understood regardless of what your background of learning is. You simply have to be able to tell how one sample of handwriting differs from another. It is in those differences that the whole science of handwriting lies.

Handwriting Charactersitics	*Personality Characteristics*
Spacing of writing	State of mind
Speed of writing	Amount of energy
Slope of writing	Degree of affection
Size of writing	Concentrative power
Line of writing	State of disposition
Terminal strokes	Degree of generosity
Capital letters	Personal tastes
Small letters	Mental development
Signature	Individuality
Flourishes	Superficialities
Style	Sharpness of mind
Margins	Sense of proportion
Pressure	Emotional state

Learn to use graphology by trying it out a little at a time until you are sure you understand how it works. You will be surprised how successful you will be after even a small amount of practice. Dealing with the details will automatically give you the confidence to complete a full scale analysis.

Remember, after a bricklayer has mastered the skill of laying bricks, one brick at a time, there is no limit to the number of bricks he can lay.

Graphology has the same unlimited possibilities once the art of analysis has been achieved.

HOW TO GET STARTED ANALYZING HANDWRITING

How to select a proper handwriting specimen

For a quick picture of an individual's personality all you need is any scrap of his handwriting. It can be in pen or pencil. It can be a signature on the list of groceries on a shopping list. What you will be able to find out, however, will be limited by the kind and the number of your handwriting samples.

The 10 rules for analyzing handwriting

To make a scientific analysis of a person's writing you should follow these simple rules:

1. Do not use a single sample of writing, but use two or three samples, and preferably these should be written a few months apart.

2. Use handwriting written in ink, if possible.

3. Do not use writing which was especially penned to be analyzed.

4. Do not use addresses written on envelopes since the writing will not be natural. Extra muscular control is generally excercised to make the writing clear and legible so that letter does not go astray.

5. Use handwriting written on unlined paper so that base lines will follow the writer's style and spacing will fit the intent of the person writing.

6. Each handwriting specimen should be long enough to contain all the letters of the alphabet, a good assortment of capitals, enough line of writing to judge spacing and style, and plenty of t-crossing and i-dots to establish supporting evidence in one direction or another.

7. Use handwriting which is as recent as possible.

8. Do not look for certain signs in writing to back up what you 'know' about an individual. What you 'know' may not be correct. The handwriting will reveal the truth.

9. When you are doing a spur-of-the-moment analysis of someone's writing, ask the person to do the following:

(a) Write his full name.

(b) Write a sentence about the weather, such as: 'It is very warm out today'.

(c) Write something personal, such as: 'I like to play gold'.

(d) Write the alphabets in capital letters.

(e) List the numbers from one to ten.

10. Under no circumstances pay any attention to what people say about themselves when they are being analyzed, not try to work the context of any written material into your analysis, complete objectivity is necessary for an accurate analysis.

Make a record

After you have selected an adequate handwriting sample, check it for the details. This will force you to examine the writing for all the important features of the script which otherwise you might overlook, especially when you make your first few handwriting studies.

In the 'Special Feature' part of the blank where there is a space after each capital letter, use the space only where you find significantly different capital letters, and then draw a facsimile of the capital letter for later interpretation. The purpose of the Graphological Record blank is to systematize your handwriting analysis. It provides you with a permanent record for quick reference or comparison at a later date, should you make another analysis of the same person. Also, if you make enough records of the same handwriting over a period of years you will build up a chronological handwriting history of the person analyzed.

The Record blank will also make it simpler for you to refer to the personality Type section since you will have a summary of the handwriting features before you for ready use. They can be checked off as you try certain signs for possible type classification.

Your next job is to find out what the various graphological signs means and then write them down on a sheet of paper as you discover them. When you see that two or more details of the writing suggest the same personality or character trait, add a check after the characteristic concerned, keeping in mind that each check is that much more supporting evidence of the existence of that trait in the individual under study.

Set yourself straight on these important points

Before proceeding any further it would be wise to set yourself straight on some general misconceptions concerning handwriting analysis as well as provide you with some special and very necessary graphological and psychological information.

Some people are so involved with the writing movement when they write that they subconsciously picture themselves as they write. They will draw a subtle picture of their physical appearance. Tallness, shortness, and either an overweight or under-weight condition are often set down in script.

Very tall people write small letters which are very tall.

Short, stocky people will fashion their small letters shorter than usual.

Persons of average weight will write a medium-pressured script.

Over-weight people will write a heavy pressured signature.

Under-weight persons will write a light-pressured signature.

There's no such thing as poor or good writing

When you are analyzing handwriting, remember that there is no such thing as 'poor' writing and 'good' writing. The more a handwriting departs from the plain letter-forms learned in school, the more does it indicates the individuality of the writer. Since individuality may be good or bad, the writing is neither one nor the other. There are 'smart' criminals and 'stupid' citizens, as well as the usual kind in each group.

Determining the sex of the writer

You cannot be absolutely certain of the sex of a writer since most people are blinds of masculinity and feminity, and will write according to their individual combinations. However, female writing will be prettier to look at, more rhythmic and decorative, as well as penned with a lighter pressure than that of a male. The masculine writer will write plainly, use a heavy pressure, and will shade his letter strokes. His t-crossings will generally be firm, full pressured, and long. Hooks, underlines, and periodic places where pressure is increased are some other signs of masculinity.

How to tell the age of the writer

Age in handwriting cannot be determined with certainty, but it can often be arrived at by a comparative analysis using rhythm, pressure, maturity of letter formations, and spacing. Poor rhythm means either a young person or a very old person. Simple letter styles suggest youth; involved or flourished letters point to a person at least over 21. Light pressure, if continuous and rhythmic, suggests a young individual. A light but broken pressure indicates a middle-aged person or older.

Health factors revealed in writing

Your state of health will affect your handwriting. If you are in good health your writing will be smooth and rhythmic. There will be no interrupted strokes. Poor health will disturb your usual way of writing.

If you write with a light pressure you will be most susceptible to eye trouble, heart disease, and tuberculosis. Heavy pressured writers will be most susceptible to diseases of the bowels and kidneys.

Near sighted people will always begin a line of writing so that it slants at a different angle from the one preceding it. In addition, the line of writing will be uneven.

Deficiencies in a person's breathing organs are shown in handwriting by the presence of rifts or catches in the loops and curves above the line. Heart trouble is evidenced by breaks in the writing, especially in the tops of the small I's and h's.

Abdominal diseases are displayed in the script of a person who makes his small p and g with crippled lower portions.

Spotting the abnormal person

You will have little trouble in picking out the abnormal individual from his handwriting. The writing will appear abnormal. Generally speaking, the writing will be extreme in one way or another. Large writing will become extra large, small writing will be almost microscopic; pressure will be muddy, heavy, and crude, or so light the pen barely marks the paper; capital letters will be almost single strokes or they will be surrounded with onion ring circles or ornate flourishes. Underlines will be repeated by numerous underscrores beneath a signature, lines of writing will run into each other in a wild, uncontrolled entanglement, and all the other normal ways, of writing will be either magnified or almost neglected. The kind and degree of abnormality will determine the way the writing will reveal it.

Differences caused by types of writing instruments

In making an analysis you should make note of the limitations embodied in the use of different kinds of writing instruments. Pencil writing will not reveal pressure properly. Steel pen script will show stroke shading which may not be typical of the regular writing. A cheap fountain pen may suggest disturbances in rhythm when actually the writer had difficulty in keeping the ink flowing easily.

A ball point pen will falsely show heavy pressure, even with light-pressured writers. Hence, before making an analysis you should find out what type of writing device was used.

Using the Grapho-Guides

The purpose of the "Grapho-Guides" is to make it possible for you to get a quick look at the personality of the writer in question. Once you are familiar with them you will realize their chief usefulness and their apparent limitations. Run your handwriting sample through the complete set for an over-all character pattern.

Have fun with handwriting

Don't worry about what you find out, either about yourself or others. Decide to be happy and constructive in your approach to this new fund of psychological knowledge. If you find deficiencies in your own character, the next step is to act in such a way that they will be corrected in due time. What you come across in other people's personalities in the way of faults can be noted with the possibility of your helping them, at least by a visible attitude of understanding.

Further on in this book you will find opportunities to classify yourself and others into personality types. There is also a section dealing entirely with the plain facts of Graphology, as distinct from the newer teachings of psychographology. The mastery of the information contained in this division is necessary before you can get the most out of analyzing characters from handwriting. Once you have this material absorbed you will be able to advance down the road of any of the fields of modern applied psychology.

Summary

Obviously, the suggestions made in this chapter illustrating ways to analyze yourself and others through your handwriting are only scratches on the surface. The more you find out about the variations in personality patterns the more you will want to know. There is actually no limit to the scope and depth of self-analysis through handwriting study and its practical application in living and working with other people. As long as you remain interested in other people you will find satisfaction in being able to look at specimens of their handwriting and finding out what their personalities are like. You can continuously use this hidden knowledge about others to make your life happier through an understanding of your fellow humans.

Use the "Grapho-Guides" to get a general picture of people and the personality type section to classify people. The Graphology section, complete with the basic principles of handwriting analysis, can be skimmed over in your first reading and referred to later as the occasion demands.

GRAPHO-GUIDES

Run a sample of your handwriting through these Grapho-Guides for a quick picture of your personality.

MATURITY SCALE

Explanation

The root of some of your unhappiness may be in the fact that you are not mature enough to adjust easily to unpleasant situations. You are still holding on to childish traits, such as feeling sorry for yourself, "blowing your top", evading issues instead of facing them, and bragging about your accomplishments.

The chart below will not tell you very much in a detailed way but it will indicate just how far advanced you are on the Maturity Scale.

Childish Writing

Rounded small m's and n's

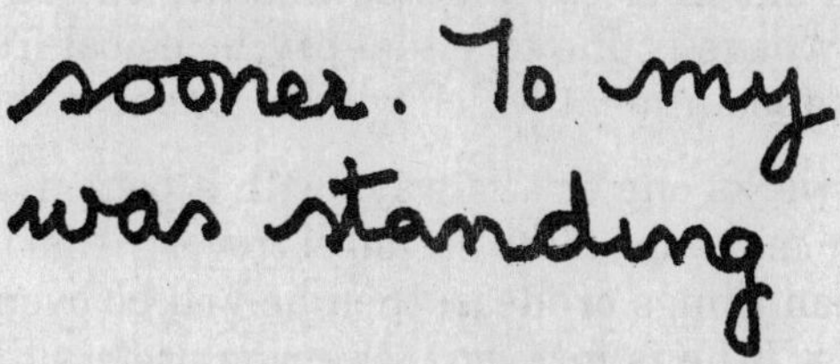

Mature Writing

Angular m's and n's.

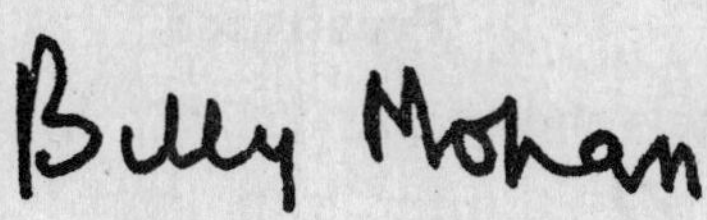

WHAT IT ALL MEANS

Childish

1. If this is the writing of a youngster of 14 or less, it means he is undergoing the normal process of growing up and is proceeding normally.
2. If it is an adult's writing, he is emotionally unstable, has neurotic tendencies, and is apt to be lazy.
3. Must be taught to be a good citizen.
4. Drives his car with little regard for other people.

Mature

1. Master of his environment.
2. Makes his own decisions.
3. Has ability to understand other person's viewpoint.
4. Enjoys being a good citizen.
5. Undertakes and practices courteous and considerate driving.

FRUSTRATION FINDER

Explanation

You can find out in a few minutes whether or not, that frustrated feeling you may have is due to actual psychological frustration or if it is just plain disappointment which will be gone in a short time.

Frustration works one or two ways with a person, depending upon his personality makeup. If he is an extrovert, that is, if he enjoys people more than things or ideas, then he will be overly-expressive in his handwriting. If he is introvert, one who prefers his own company to that of others, he will be more intense in penning his script.

Any disturbance in rhythm also indicates frustration.

Frustrated

Exaggerated Capitals and Loops.

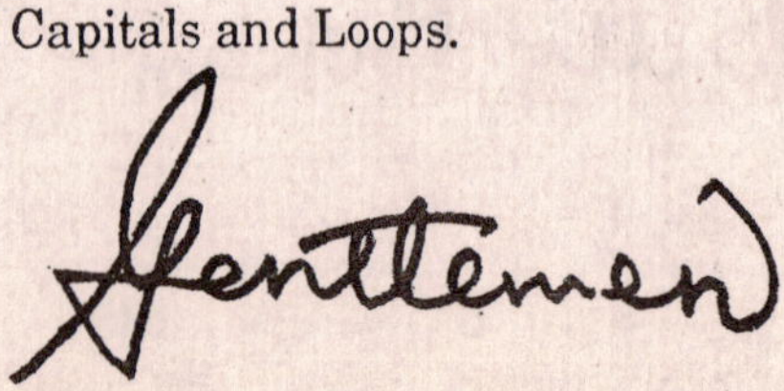

Extremely small and heavy-pressured writing.

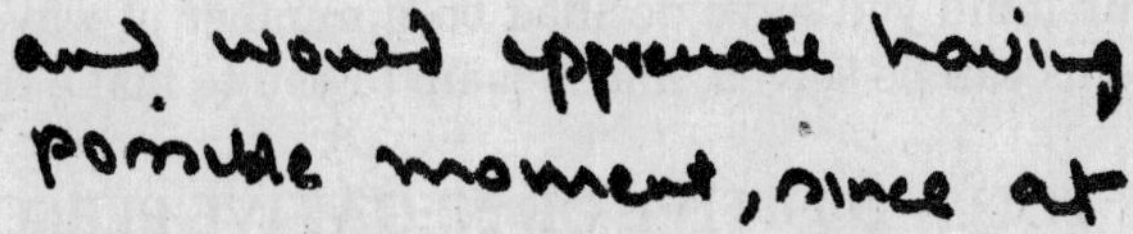

Not Frustrated

Capitals not more than three times as tall as small letters.

Small writing with normal pressure.

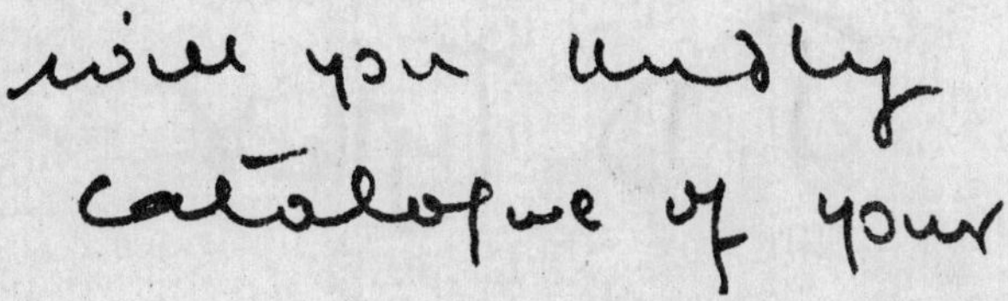

WHAT IT ALL MEANS

Frustrated

1. When you are frustrated you are not able to use your normal nervous energy along lines that your personality want to. You have a feeling of being blocked at every turn. In most cases it has a definite connection with affection of one kind or another.
2. You can overcome frustration by simply setting out and doing the things that will make you happy.

Not Frustrated

1. You have a normal and happy sex life, or the prospect of one.
2. In your mind you have decided on a number of ways that your problems can be solved, and it is up to you to make the choice.

ARE YOU A POSITIVE OR NEGATIVE PERSON?

Explanation

Positive people are welcomed everywhere because they are outgoing in their living. They may be good or bad, but atleast they are meeting life head-on and are fitting themselves, their own way, into the human family.

Negative people repel us because they withdraw from life, show coldness toward other people, and generally give the impression that it is not necessary to be expressive towards us.

Obviously, it is best to be positiver. Which are you?

Positive People Write Large

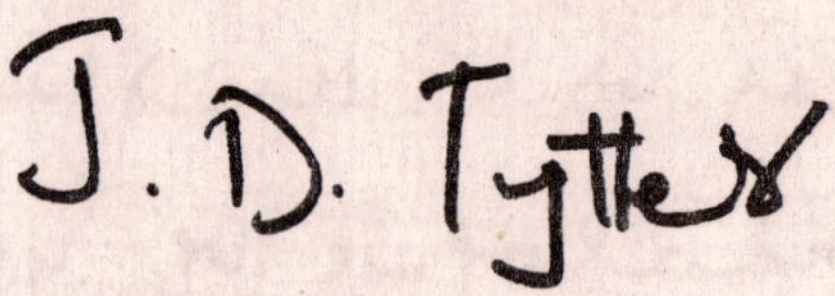

Negative People Write Small

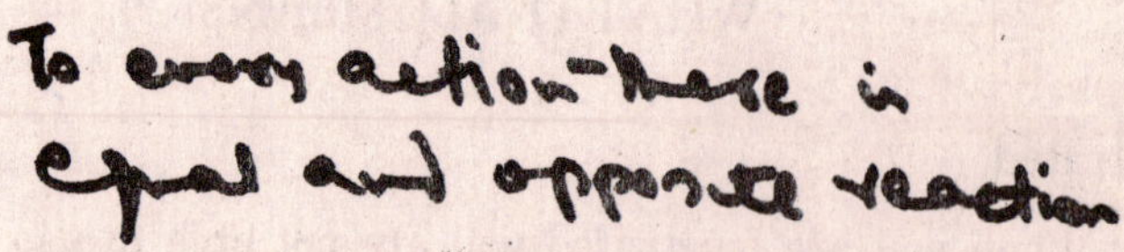

HOW IS YOUR SELF-RESPECT?

It is very important that you maintain your self-respect if you wish to be happy. You must think well of yourself or you cannot expect others to think well of you. People will invariably judge your worth by the value you set on yourself.

You must think well of yourself, but not so well that it is an inflated estimate. Likewise you should never feel inferior. You are as human as anyone else. What better common denominator could you have?

1. If your Capital I is smaller in size than the rest of your capitals, then you do not believe in yourself sufficiently.

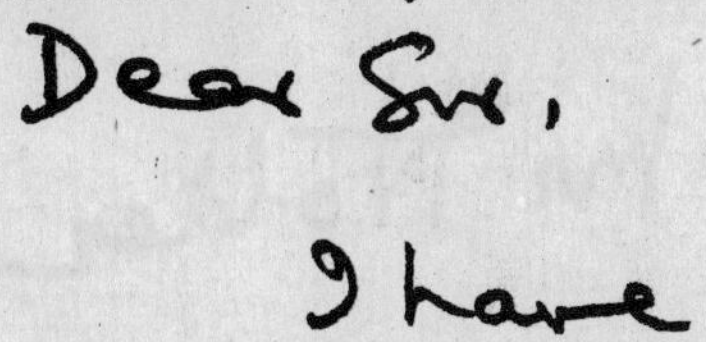

2. If your Capital I is the same size or slightly larger than your other capitals, then you have a reasonable self-respect.

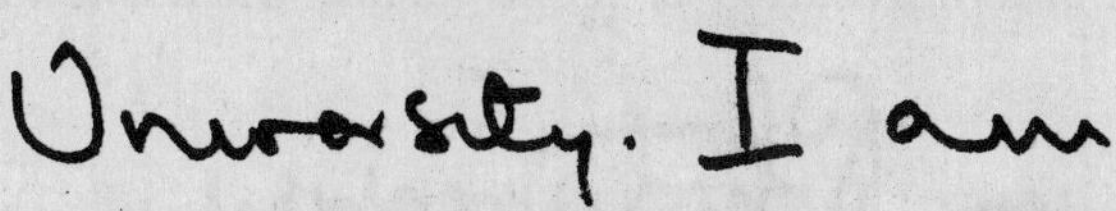

3. If your Capital I is much larger than the other Capitals, your self-esteem is exaggerated and you will be conceited. If you are an out-going person as well, you will tend to annoy other people, hence this is a trait to tone down if you have it.

ARE YOU ORIGINAL, ORDINARY OR ODD?

The general style of your handwriting will tell you if you are original and creative or if you merely imitate or copy other people or their ideas. It will also point you out as peculiar or eccentric.

Most people in the world are average in the amount of originality they possess. The truly original amount to only a small percentage of the population. The creative persons generally take the leadership, at least in the local situations in which they are concerned. The ordinary citizen steps into line and follows.

Eccentric individuals are even fewer than the original persons. We call them "odd", "queer", "unusual" or "different". Sometimes their eccentricity is masked as originality and their leadership is inflicted upon the whole nation who are asked to rally their "new" ideas.

1. Ordinary........Writing formed the same as taught in school.

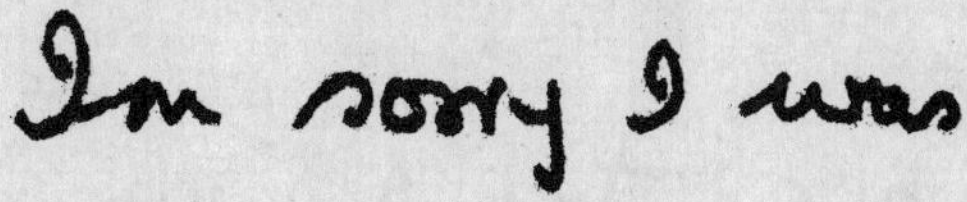

2. Original........Original letter forms, especially capitals.

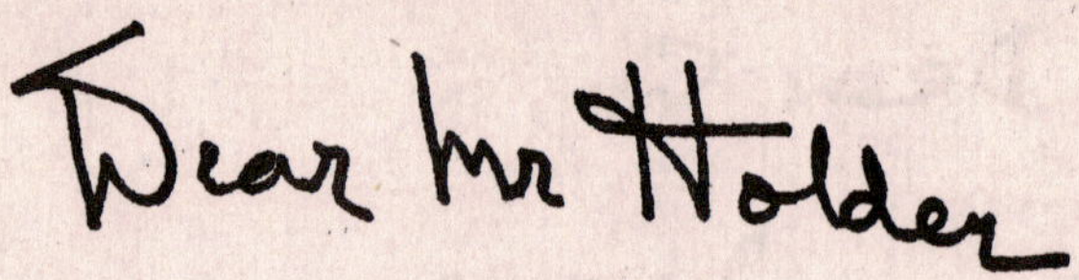

3. Odd...........Exaggeration of letter forms, with a tendency to be ornate.

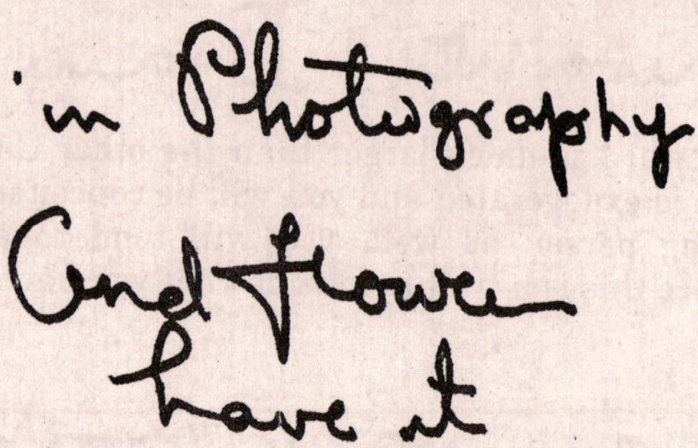

Note: An "odd" person may be a genius, mentally ill or a mental defective, a criminal, or merely a person who has limited his creativity to one phase of life, thus calling public attention to his originality by its very extravagance.

HOW IS YOUR DRIVE?

Success in life is strongly dependent upon the amount of useful energy you can muster up to meet each day's demands. It is more than a matter of simple good health. It is more a possession of what psychologists call "drive".

You may have ambition, but you must also have the power—house of dogged determination to energize your mind into action. Strong energy in motion is drive.

A quick study of the pressures of your writing will tell you how much drive you can claim.

1. Light Pressure. Completely lacking in drive.

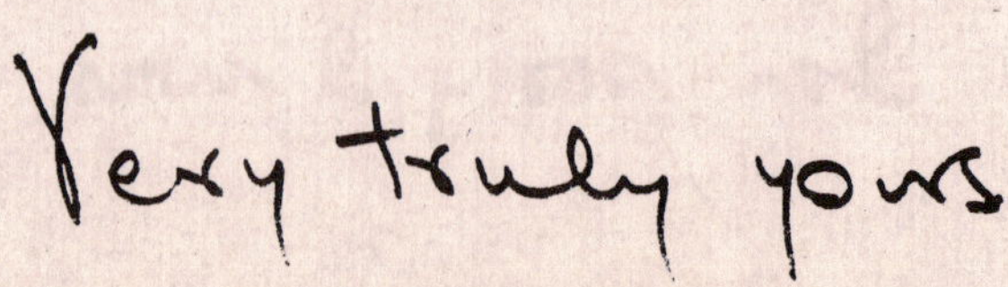

2. Medium Pressure. Average drive. Mildly successful.

3. Heavy pressure. Strong Drive. Highly successful in anything tried.

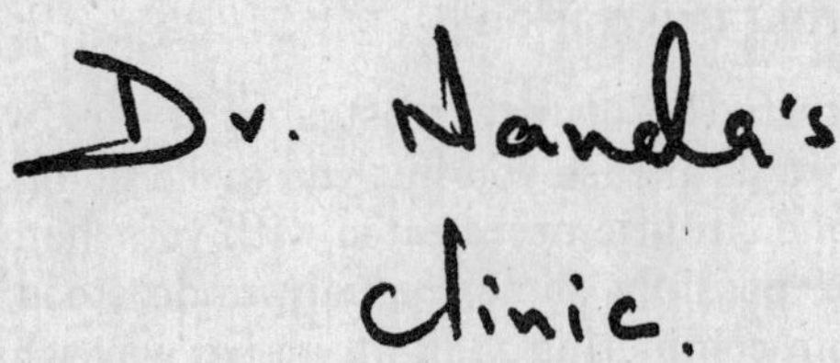

Special note

(a) Add hooks to heavy pressure and your drive turns to irritating aggressiveness which will interfere with your full success.

(b) Add over-size capital letters and your drive becomes selective and you become selfish and self-centered. You will be successful but you will be not be very happy because of the many people you will have "stepped upon" in your climb to the top.

HOW TO ANALYZE YOURSELF THROUGH YOUR HANDWRITING

What Kind of personality do you have?

Now you can study your handwriting and discover the kind of personality that you have. Since there are literally hundreds of ways of classifying people, that is exactly the approach that has been taken in this book. Using the information compiled in these pages you will be able to look at yourself in so many different ways and in so many varying lights that you will certainly end up with an accurate and inclusive portrait of yourself. The analysis will cost you nothing, but it may mean a fortune to you if you use this valuable new knowledge wisely.

Are you over-aggressive towards others?

We live in a civilization marked by aggression. Some people have allowed the spriit of our age to make them over-aggressive. If you are too aggressive, you will be distasteful to many persons you meet and this will interfere with your achievements, success, and other advancements. Check your writing for aggressive tendencies, such as, an extreme forward slant, angular letter forms, heavy pressure, heavily-shaded style of writing, lance-like to-crossings, and your ending strokes carried almost straight down instead of finishing straight out or curled upward.

Free yourself from frustration

Why be frustrated? You are frustrated if you would like to do something that would please you but you avoid doing it because some other person, some situation connected with your home habits or your work routine, or possibly some vaguely understood restrictive fear prevents you from completing it in an active way what in your mind you are certain is a pleasant bit of behaviour. You should not be frustrated if there is a way to escape from this mental jail. Frustration is an attitude of mind and as such can be changed. If you know you can get rid of frustrated feelings you have made a begining in freeing yourself.

The sad reality about frustrated people is that one tiny frustration encourages other frustrations until these persons are sour, unhappy bundles of unsatisfied longings.

The only way to get rid of frustrated feelings is to start doing what you think you cannot do. If it turns out that you really are not able to do it successfully you will no longer worry about it. If you get real satisfaction from your activity you will have found new personal freedom.

The signs of a frustrated personality

Observe your writing for the following signs of frustrated personality. One sign means at least some frustration is present in your life; if all signs are seen in your writing you should start this very minute to fight your way through to freedom.

1. Cramped, small writing.
2. t-bars short, even-pressured, and crossed low on the stem.

3. Hooks, catches, and backward movements in writing.
4. Backhand writing combined with heavy-pressured small writing.
5. Narrow, close writing in a large hand.
6. Printed writing in a small hand, combined with heavy pressure.
7. Vertical writing in a medium hand combined with large, flourshing capitals.
8. Capital I made with a single stroke, heavy-pressured.
9. Small letters tied with tight knots.
10. Small a's and o's tightly closed.
11. Signature encircled with a large loop.

Your fears may be without foundation

When fear becomes major factor in colouring an individual's personality it needs to be studies so that it can be unseated from its place of dominance. Your handwriting will reveal just how afraid you are, and this may be a segment of psychological knowledge that you may not have been aware of. You may have attributed your fearful way of living to some other cause, a cause which you may have told yourself you could not help or control.

Before examining your writing, let us take a swift trip into the realm of fear. In its mildest form, fear is doubt. In its most frightful form it is terror. Between these extremes we have the feelings of misery, nervousness, confused excitment, insecurity, inadequacy, and like emotions or emotional reactions. Because fear is an emotion, it is induced either by ourselves or by a fear-stimulating environment.

Fears which you create yourself can be stopped by yourself. It may be difficult to remove fears produced by your environment. By removing the environment, or by taking yourself away from the environment, you can even erase these fears.

Most fears, of any sort, are unfounded. There are many fears based on sheer ignorance. Knowledge will remove them. Misconceptions breed scores of fears which clear-minded people are never bothered by. Narrowness of mind, or the inability to put ourselves in the other person's place, causes another group of unfounded fears. Insults to our own built-up ego may bring on a whole series of unjustified anxieties. Sex rivalry even stimulates some persons to be afraid.

Characteristics of fear in handwriting

If your handwriting reveals any of the following characteristics you will be subject to one or more bad effects of unfounded fear.

1. Poor rhythm in writing, suggesting lack of muscular coordination.
2. Uncontrolled variation in pen pressure.
3. Extreme variations in size of small letters.
4. Any expression of nervousness in writing, from "loose nerves" resulting in undue lightening of pressure, to "tight nerves" causing sudden intensification of pressure.
5. Inability to hold a pen steady enough to write a complete sentence.

Some Special advice on fear for certain kinds of people

1. If you write a vertical hand, indicating reserve and possible timidity, you should practice doing some of the things you have in the past been afraid to do. Get rid of the fear habit.

2. If you write with original letter formations and flourished capitals, you have a tendency to fear the imaginary, which is a sheer waste of time. Your lively and reactive personality will prevent you from removing fear entirely, but you should confine your fears to those which are real.

3. If you write with an uneven base line and if you vary your small letters too much, you mostly fear insecutity. Strive for security and thus get rid of a prime cause of your unhappiness.

4. If you write with a heavy-pressured angular hand, with lancelike t-crossings, you have the bad habit of reacting to fear by wanting to fight. Keep your emotions under control and you will suffer no ill effects.

5. If you have a lot of hooks in your handwriting, you allow each new fear to stir up old fears, thus multiplying your anxieties. Live with your fears one at a time and you will be able to handle them better.

6. If you write a conventional, unoriginal hand with the capitals made so simple they are almost print-like, you are in a continual state of a dread of the unknown. You anticipate fear. You should save your anticipation for pleasant experiences and soon there will be nothing to fear.

Check yourself for these likeable personality qualities

1. Sincerity	Straight lines; small letters of equal size ungraceful hand; letters in words increase in size occasionally.
2. Spontaneity	Down strokes shaded; upper strokes long; cross strokes never descending.
3. Friendliness	Letters extended; m and n like w and u.
4. Dependability	Straight lines; letters all same size.
5. Determination	Long, firm t-bars; lower loop letters ending in strokes instead of loops.
6. Adaptability	Uneven base line; angular writing.
7. Conversational Ease	Smooth-running hand; d and t looped.
8. Broad-mindedness	Words and lines well-spaced.

People will dislike you if you possess these qualities

1. Insincerity	Decreasing size of letters in words; hasty writing in backhand style.
2. Dishonesty	Small a and o open at the bottom; uneven line of writing.
3. Carelessness	Loop letters of one line running into lines above and below; careless punctuation; t's crossed many ways and carelessly.
4. Coldness (Emotional coolness)	Backhand writing in the angular hand; writing medium or in size; light-pressured writing tending toward conventional letter forms.
5. Weakness of will	t's crossed very lightly; i's dotted with comma like mark instead of dot.

6. Narrowmindedness	Words close together; crowded spacing; letters never extended.
7. Stinginess	Angular, crowded writing. All letter small; terminal strokes absent.
8. Licentiousness	Muddy, pasty-looking, heavy writing; strokes coarse and irregular.

Watch out for emotional storm warnings

Your handwriting is your own personal barometer for emotional storm warnings. The pressure in your script will change according to rise or fall of your feelings. You have perhaps noticed that when you dash off a note in anger you write faster than usual. A closer examination will reveal to you that you also increase the pen pressure. In addition, t-crossings will be made longer than usual, i-dots will be made like commas, and rightward-leaning writing will take on a greater slant.

When you observe that your pressure is consistently getting heavier, you can be sure that your emotions are begining to influence your daily activities to a larger degree. It also means that there will be an increase in stress and strain, thus making it easier for you to become mentally or physically ill. Tenseness will take over as logical reasoning is relegated to the background. The remedy for this danger is to take more time out for reflective thinking to give you ample opportunity for taking stock of yourself. You need to slow yourself down to prevent your emotions from racing you ahead.

Emotions need add colour to living, but when they are not controlled they only confuse.

Increase in pressure to the point of heaviness also indicates over-emphasis on material things such as the acquisition of money and taking one's work too seriously.

The lighter your pen pressure the healthier you are liable to be. If your pressure varies from day to day between light and heavy you need someone's help to get you back on an even keel.

Summary

In analyzing yourself you must believe what you find out about yourself from your handwriting. You must also decide to do something about correcting any faults you discover. You will find life pleasanter when you know how you look to other people, seeing behind your own personal prejudices. Foolish mental fogs caused by frustrations and fears will disappear and life will be brighter as you get a clear picture of life's interesting relationships.

Happiness was meant for you, regardless of your station or condition. Knowing yourself truly will enrich your own mental outlook. Knowing what the rest of your friends and associates are like will enable you to live with them easily because you will understand them as individuals and you will be able to adjust to them as individuals. You will be accepted everywhere. Who could dislike a person who understood him better than he knew himself?

GRAPHOLOGY: THE MEANINGS IN THE DIFFERENT WAYS THAT PEOPLE WRITE

Graphology, or handwriting analysis, as it is more popularly known, is the science of discovering a person's character and personality by examining his handwriting. European countries, notably France and England, accept the testimony of graphologists as legitimate court evidence, thereby giving the science authority. In some of the European universities, Graphology is listed as one of the subjects taught, and in our own country numerous experiments have been carried on in psychological research centres to discover uses for this science in the field of personality guidance.

Raymond Trillat, of the Psycho-Pedagogic Center of the University of Paris, in addition to carrying on his career as a practicing graphologist advising business firms on personnel selection, also has been experimenting with the use of handwriting therapy to treat children for emotional ills.

Enough has been found by American experimenters and psychologists to admit the unmistakable relationship between a person's handwriting and his character.

Nothing is included in the following pages making up the graphology text which I have not personally found to be true through comparative handwriting studies and personality analysis in my 20 years experience.

Remember that the real worth of graphological material that follows is in the way you use it, with what you know about modern psychology, to improve yourself and to understand others.

This is the new science of Psychographology.

SOME BASIC PRINCIPLES OF HANDWRITING ANALYSIS

Principle of neutralization

Every handwriting will show some contradictory signs, but this should not be allowed to confuse you. Apply the principle of neutralization; that is, one graphological sign may neutralize or cancel out the effect of another graphological sign if both signs are present in equal numbers. If one sign indicates selfishness and another denotes unselfishness it means that the person possesses both characteristics in average proportions so that actually they neutralize each other. If a person's script shows that he is both selfish and unselfish then, in reality, he is neither. Strongly selfish and heroically unselfish individuals will not write average hands but will write according to their character.

Principle of support

When a person is strongly endowed with a particular character trait there will be two or more signs in the handwriting indicating this fact. This is knwon as the principle of support. The more signs that are present tending to support the existence of a trait of character, the stronger is that particular trait. Strong traits are usually habitual with a person whereas weak traits are displayed only occasionally.

If the weak trait is a flattering one then it is displayed only when the person possessing it is in a very good humour, most always when everything is going his way. If the weak trait is a derogatory one then it is displayed only when the person having it loses control of his feelings, that is, when he is angry or unduly excited.

SOME SECRETS OF SLANT

Forward movement

When a person writes with his handwriting slanting to the right he is executing a natural movement or gesture. He is allowing himself full expression, working freely with no restrictions. That is why a person who writes like that is natural and sympathetic. He leans out towards others and is quite apt to be emotional since he allows his feelings to direct him.

Handwriting sloping to the right would also indicate that the person writing in that manner would be the kind who would like to express himself. He would allow his emotions to dictate his actions. The more his handwriting slanted to the right the more he would be liable to let himself go. People who freely express themselves are often very demonstrative in their affections since that is their way of satisfying the basic need of love.

Movement and emotion

The continuous action which natural and free expression necessitates tends to discourage an emotionally excited person from calming his emotions once they have been aroused. This is true because it is difficult to stop when one is moving forward at a steady, swift, and rhythmic pace. Regardless of what he is doing, if a person is filled with ardour and enthusiasm, he will find it hard to stop when he is being carried along on the swift current of his emotions.

A Natural person responds readily

A natural person is more open to suggestion than one who is unnatural because a natural person does not set up any artificial barriers or objections that might neutralize or turn aside another's suggestions.

Forward-writing people are easily made to do things since their naturalness places them in a mood favourable for starting at the slightest suggestion. Natural people take others at their word, falling prey to propaganda pleas, believing all advertising, and judging the world by the way it appears to them.

Unrestrained feelings will over-rule reason

People who allow themselves complete and full expression of their emotions are apt to be swayed to decisions by their feelings and not by their reasoning powers.

The most natural way of life is to be guided by your feelings since this is most in accordance with the nature that is all about us. The vivilized reasoning ability that we are all so proud of was developed by experience and has led more and more to unnaturalness and artificiality as we have progressed in reasoning things out. As we think we tend to act, with man always delighting to disagree with nature and acting in his own chosen way. Man was guided by his reason when he constructed factories; were he directed by his feelings he might have been content to remain in the agricultural state.

People who are very expressive emotionally write with a very decided rightward slant, picturing in their handwriting the excess of freedom that they crave and yield to.

Self-control in writing

If to write with a forward slant to one's writing is the most natural and also the easiest way to write, then writing that is vertical must be the result of a conscious control on the part of the writer. He deliberately keeps himself from writing naturally. This act of his is prompted by an inner desire to hold back his natural expression and this feeling is carried over into his handwriting.

The very fact that he is thinking about what he is doing shows that he acts not on impulse but rather as the result of deliberation. His emotions do not rule his judgments. If they did, his writing would be written with a natural, forward slope. He weighs the arguments for each action, pros and cons, rather than succumbing to sentiments.

Wiser action results from reasoning

A person who consciously controls himself from allowing his feelings to have full sway over his actions will tend to make many more right judgements than one who is ruled by impulse. People who are always "flying off the handle" and who are easily excited are apt to do things according to the dictates of their feelings, not considering their actions in the light of reason. Their judgements naturally will be warped to some degree because they will have nothing to set right their off-balance, bringing them back to an even keel. If they examined both sides of a question, as they would if they stopped to think things through, they would be able to arrive at a fair conclusion.

Actions resulting from previous thoughtful consideration are wiser than those arising from a mere impulse since the one is the balance between two divergent opinions, whereas the other can only be the way one would act if he allowed his feelings to guide him. Only one viewpoint is considered. There is no way for this viewpoint to be balanced or to be modified and if one's emotions happen to direct one's thoughts along wrong lines then the judgement will be poor.

Backhand writing

People who write backhand exercise a great deal of self restraint becuase it takes even more effort and more conscious control to write this way than to write vertically. People who write backhand usually think of themselves first and are not naturally generous.

Individuals who control their emotions so well that they only do things which their reason dictates that they may, will tend to be selfish. Backhand writers are of this sort. They know the reason for everything they do and never do anything they do not want to do. This increases their selfishness since if they only do things to benefit themselves, they will not be evaluating things from the other person's viewpoint. There are very few situations that help others just because they help us.

Writers of the backhand style also are critical because they study life's happenings with an impersonal approach. They lose the beneficial effect gained from taking a sympathetic, emotionally-coloured attitude to at least some of the day's events. Devoid of naturalness they find it difficult to meet others halfway but wait cautiously for them to make all the advances.

Warning

Handwriting reveals the true character and personality of an individual but it cannot tell you the exact details of what that individual has experienced in his lifetime. It will indicate how that person has been affected by environment and by his heredity but it will not divulge the specific nature of any past happenings or conditions.

For instance, the writing of an individual may show that he is unusually shy, but it will give no real clue as to the real cause of the shyness. By building up a composite personality picture of an individual from examining various sings seen in script you may be able to guess at the kind of situation which could have caused the shyness, but you would never be absolutely sure. For that reason, the beginner in handwriting analysis should concern himself with the use of psychographology as a useful aid to self discovery rather than as an infallible pen protrait of the past.

Everyone's life is different just as everyone's writing differs. Five hundred greedy persons have five hundred different sets of circumstances and backgrounds accoutning for their individual patterns of greediness. The psychographologist must be content with finding out the simple fact that they are greedy and then use that information in a constructive or profitable way.

When you find out all about yourself and others by looking at handwriting you will be more interested in the future of things than in historical background. Handwriting analysis cannot reveal the direction of future events except to point out the common sense conclusions apt to occur if events follow normal courses. If handwriting reveals that a person is dishonest it would be fair to assume that sooner or later that person will yield to temptation and be in trouble, more or less serious, depending upon how the situation fits in with other situations impinging upon it. A forger may pass a hundred checks and get away with each forgery, until he writes out one more check, after which he is caught simply because no one detected his forgeries in the first 100 bogus check signings.

Explanations for the pages that follow

The material in the following pages has been set down in tabular form, with illustrations situated close to the graphological explanations for convenient and quick reference. There is no need to memorize or master all of these facts. The usefulness of this organization to handwriting analysis sings is in helping you to delve into the details of graphology. With this information as a sound base you can progress to psychographology by adding what you have learned about psychology.

Slope

1. Forward slanting writing. Writing slants to the right about 45 degrees.

   Denotes a friendly, affectionate nature.

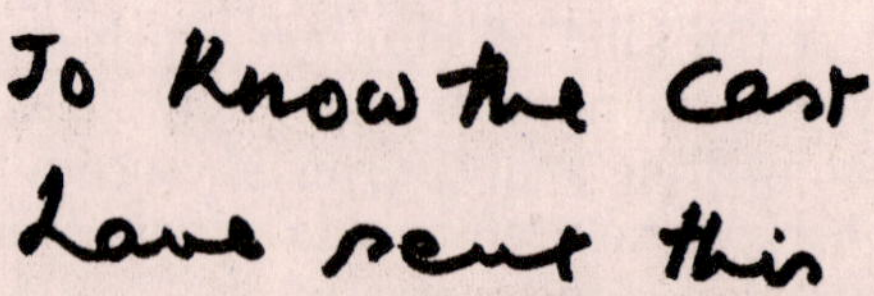

2. Forward slanting to a marked degree. Writing slants to the right as much as it possibly can without becoming horizontal.

   Denotes a person very affectionate in nature and one who places the heart before the head in most important decisions.

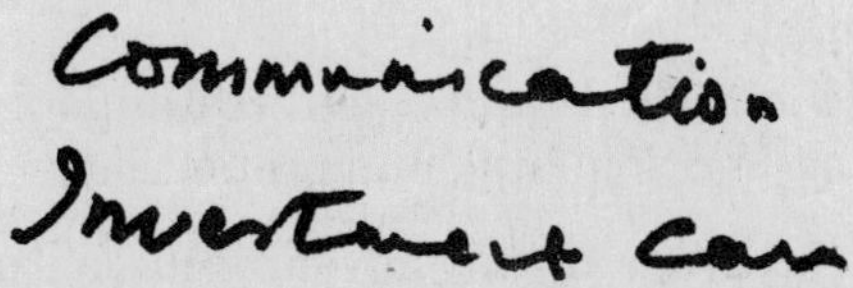

3. Vertical writing. Writing does not slant either to the left or to the right but assumes a vertical position.

Denotes a person who has a good measure of self control and who is the master of his emotions. His head rules his heart.

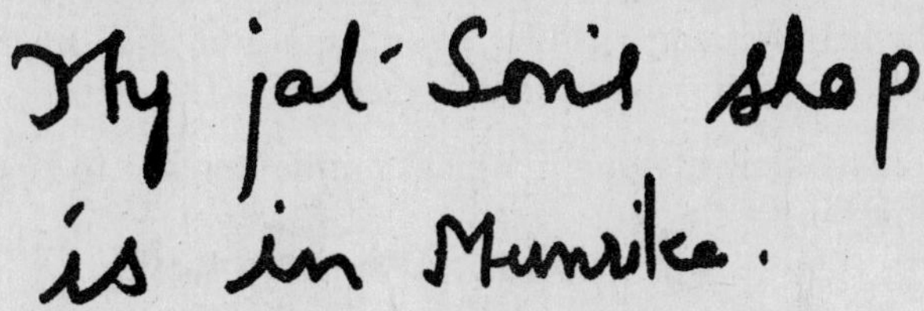

4. Backhand writing. Writing slants to the left.

Denotes a person secretive, introspective, and one not apt to be very sincere in his demonstrations of affection.

Form

1. Copybook. Almost exact copy of style of handwriting taught in school.

Denotes an imitative unoriginal nature. Commonplace personality. One with no ideas of his own.

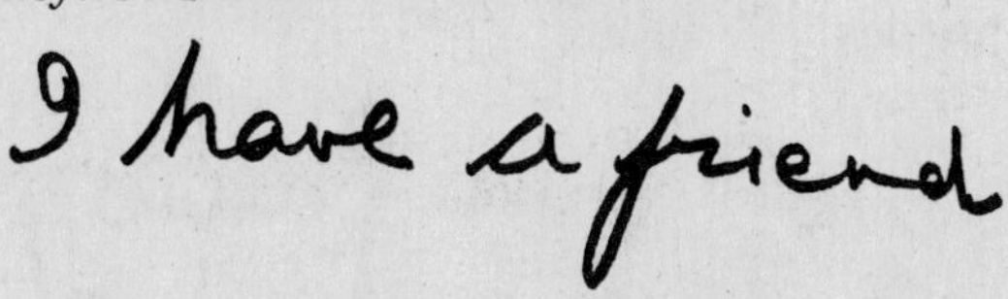

2. Conventional. Unoriginal letter formations with no attempt at any individuality.

Denotes a conventional nature. Not apt to do anything particularly outstanding. Afraid to do things on his own initiative.

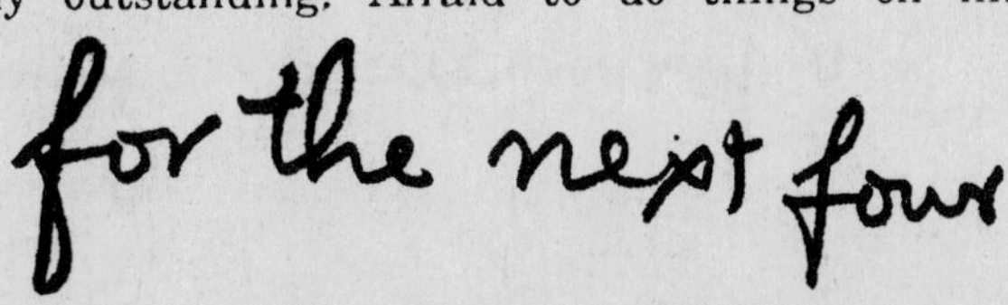

3. Flourished. Flourished capital letters and long ending strokes on small letter. Writing large and pretentious.

   Denotes an extravagant and adventurous nature. One paying little attention to details. Great imagination and self esteem.

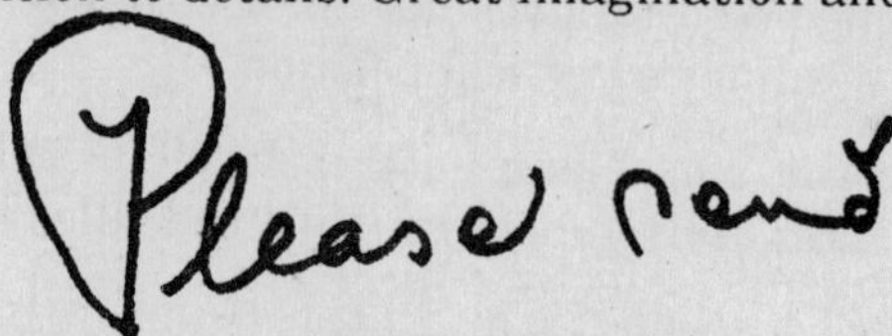

4. Awkward. Writing sprawls over page and is ill formed. Motor control of writing movement is lacking.

   Denotes a slow moving, illogical mind. One apt to be careless in his thinking.

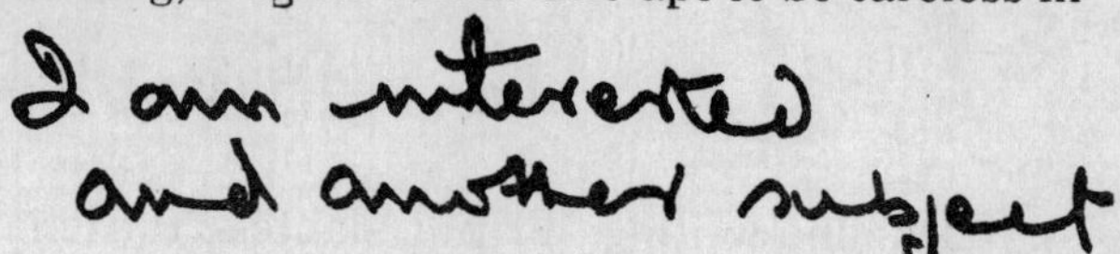

5. Ornate. Writing is dressed up with unnecessary curleycues.

   Denotes a fussy nature paying too much attention to unnecessary details.

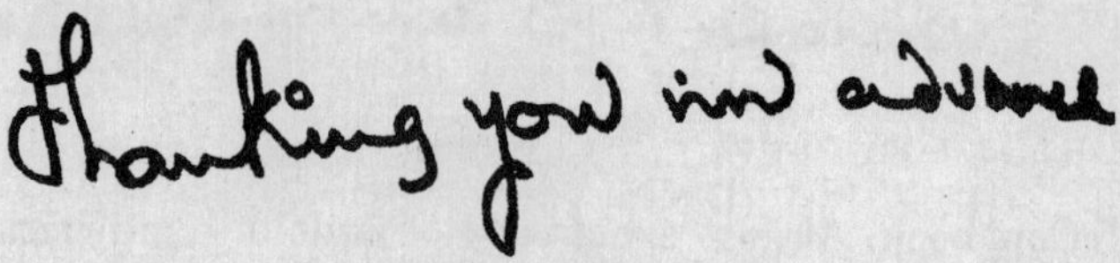

Loops

1. Loops long above line and short below.

   Denotes an idealistic nature.

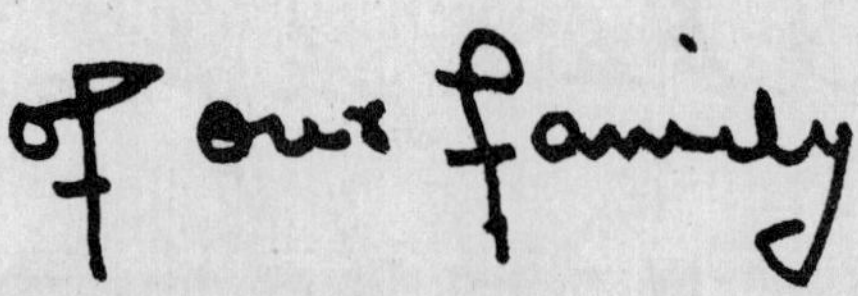

2. Loops short above line and long below.

   Denotes a businesslike, material nature.

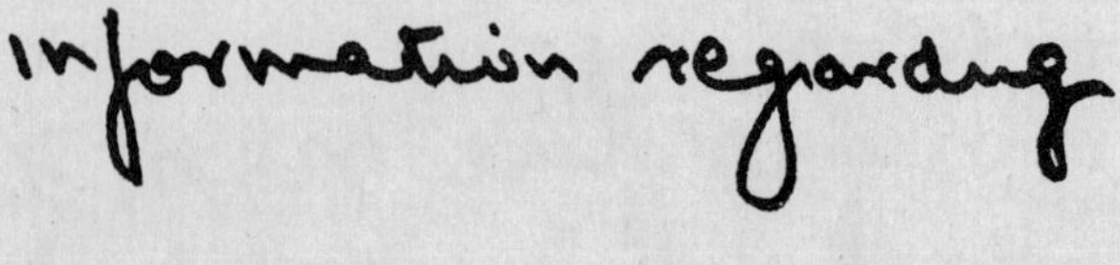

Graphology

1. Loop letters well developed both above and below line.

   Denotes a strong imagination. An enterprising nature.

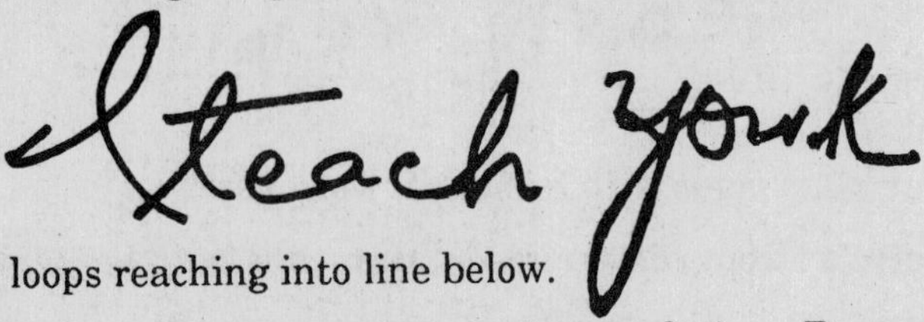

2. Lower loops reaching into line below.

   Denotes one who is restless and speculative. Romantically inclined. One fond of new ideas.

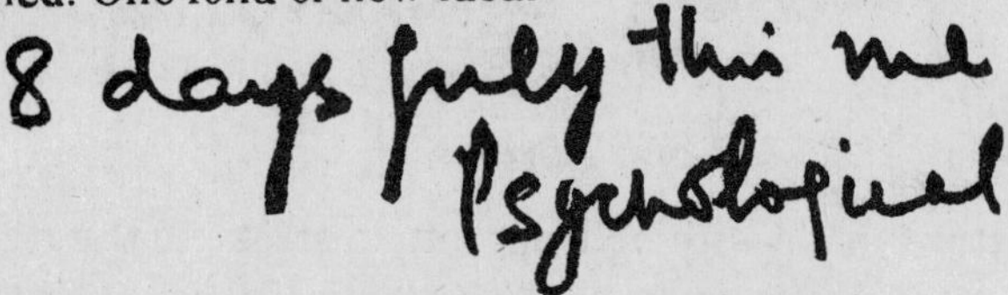

3. Upstroke of lower loop letters curve well to left.

   Denotes a clannish nature.

4. Lower loops wide and inflated.

   Denotes one gifted with imagination and cleverness.

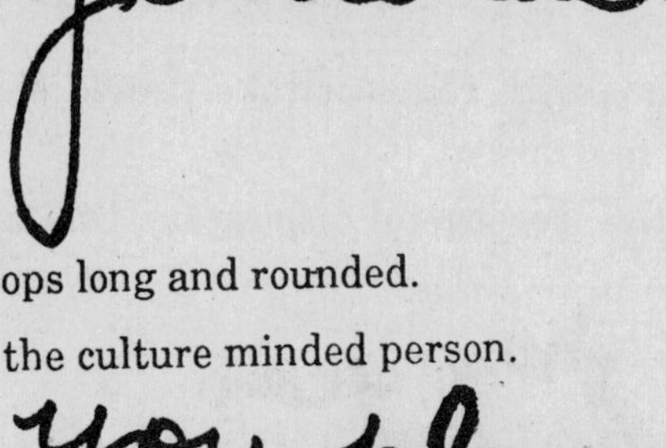

5. Lower loops long and rounded.

   Denotes the culture minded person.

6. Lower loops made with stroke.

Denotes a conservative nature. One who is practical, systematic, firm, and self reliant.

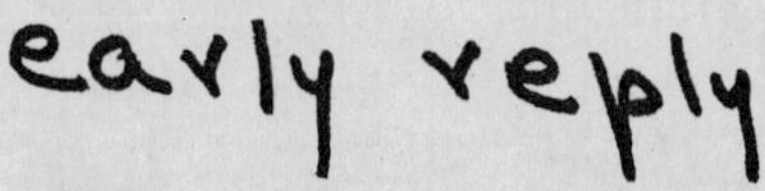

7. Lower loops made with firm, heavy strokes.

Denotes a strong, determined nature; one hard to convince.

Loop Letters

1. Small letter f made with no loop, return stroke to the right.

Denotes one desirous of getting things done quickly.

2. Small letter f made with round, inflated loops.

Denotes one fond of pleasure; a buoyant and carefree nature. One lacking in deep thought.

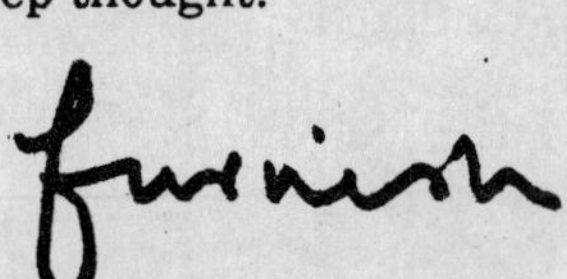

3. Small letter f made with return stroke turned sharply to the left.

Denotes a vindictive, revengeful disposition. One inclined to be lazy.

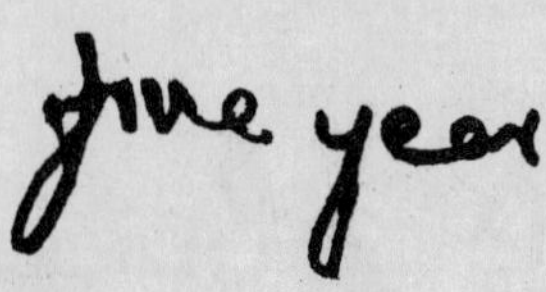

4. Small letter g made with stroke instead of loop.
   Denotes a determined mind.

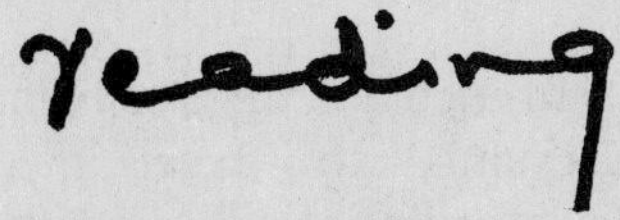

5. Small g made with return stroke to the right.
   Denotes a generous, kind nature.

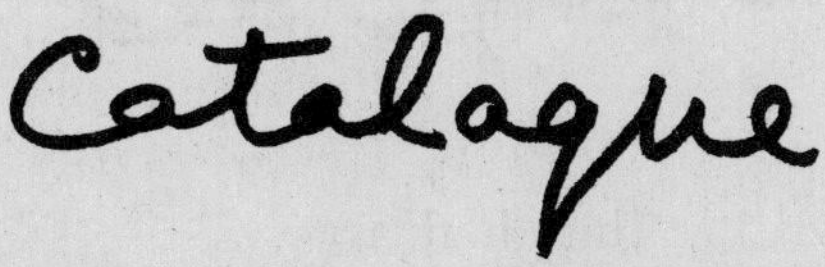

6. Loop of small g made unduly long.
   Denotes a tendency towards moral weakness.

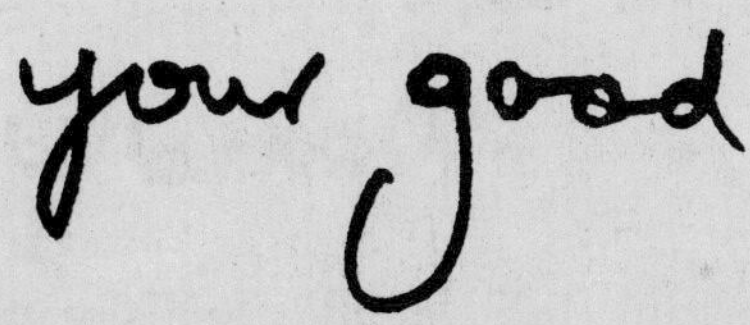

7. Small letter g and y made with flourishes within loop.
   Denotes a tendency towards moral weakness.

8. Small letters g and y end with stroke and tiny hook
   Denotes a persevering nature.

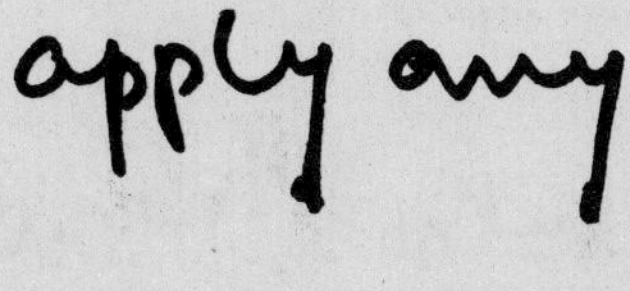

Pressure

1. Heavy pressured writing, firmly made strokes with or without shading.

Denotes one with assurance and aggressiveness. One lacking in delicacy and possessing an exacting and domineering disposition one who is selfish, vain, and inconsiderate unless refined by much education.

2. Heavy pressured writing, thick and large.

Denotes one who is deceitful and revengeful; rough and bold in deportment. Marked talents along certain lines. Self reliant.

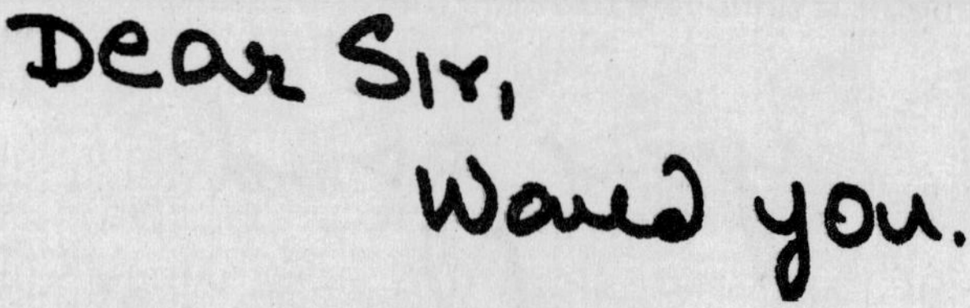

3. Heavy pressured writing, large, muddy and sloppy.

Denotes a sensual nature; one with strong passions and an animal appetite.

4. Light pressured writing, total absence of shading; all downstrokes made lightly, and without pressure.

Denotes a temperate nature; one with a quiet and simple disposition. High sense of honor. Kindly nature. One with little craving for physical pleasurs.

5. Unconsciously shaded writing;

Denotes an insistent nature. One with natural executive ability. One who desires all the good things of life and who is willing to work for them.

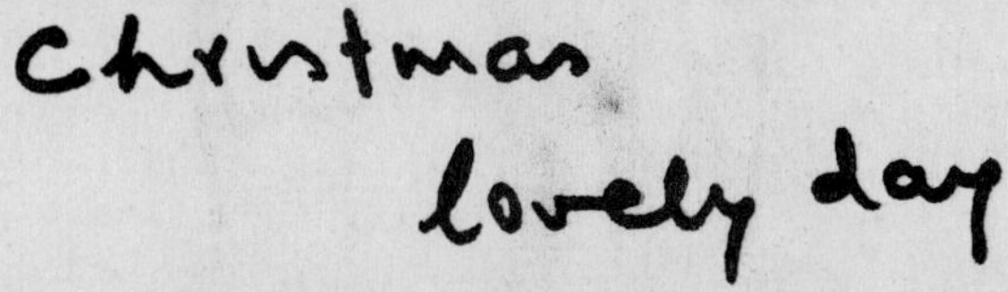

6. Consciously shaded writing, downstrokes made deliberate and heavy to make the writing beautiful.

Denotes an affected, egotistical nature. One lacking in good taste, weak in character and possessing a poor intellect.

Capitals

1. Capitals large and out of proportion to small letter. (More than three times as high)

Denotes an egotistical, conceited person. One loving display. Possessing a strong sense of pride.

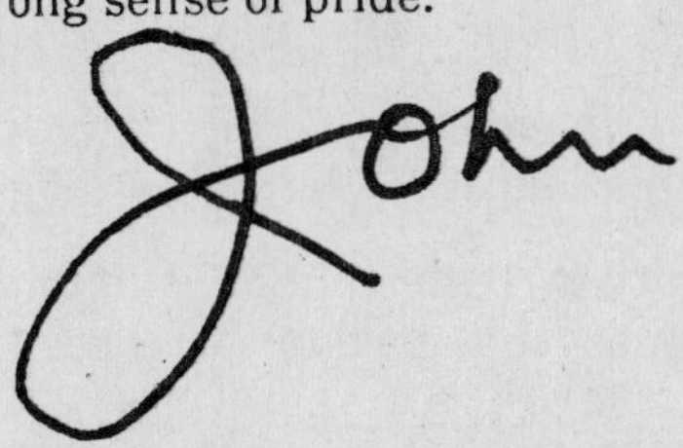

2. Capitals small—not more than twice the size of the small letter.

Denotes a timid nature; one lacking in self esteem.

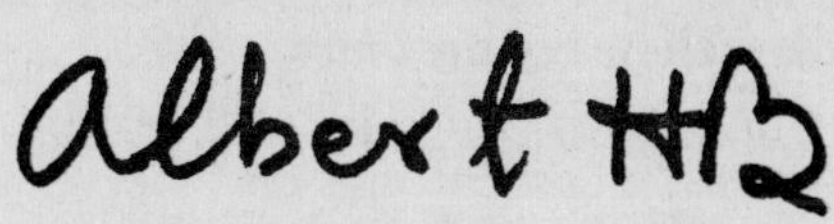

3. Capitals unusually ornamented.

Denotes one ostentatious in manner and of mediocre talents. Shallow intellect.

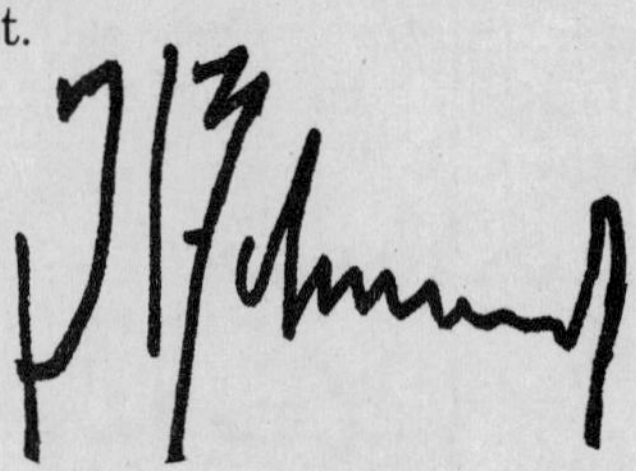

4. Capitals plain and almost printlike.

Denotes a modest, refined nature, with cultural tastes.

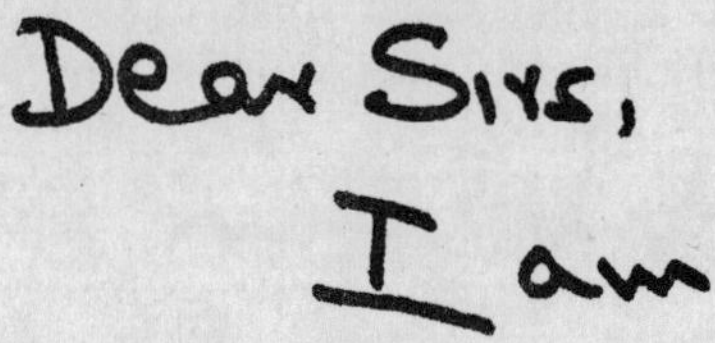

5. Capitals made plain and large.

Denotes a self reliant nature. Strong sense of personal pride.

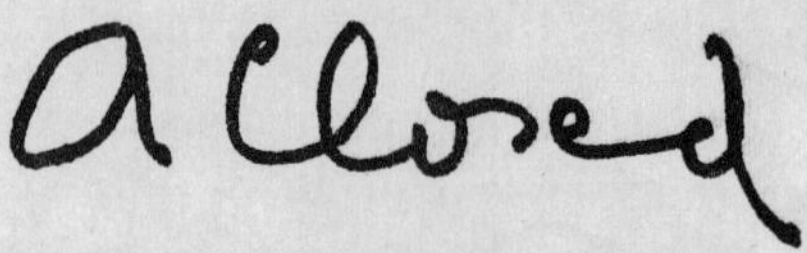

6. Incurve present in capitals. (The curve is an initial stroke preceeding the making of the letter, passing from right to left.)

Denotes one with a high opinion of himself coupled with a strong sensitiveness in regard to social position.

7. Capitals made with heavy pressure.

Denotes one loving pleasure and comfort.

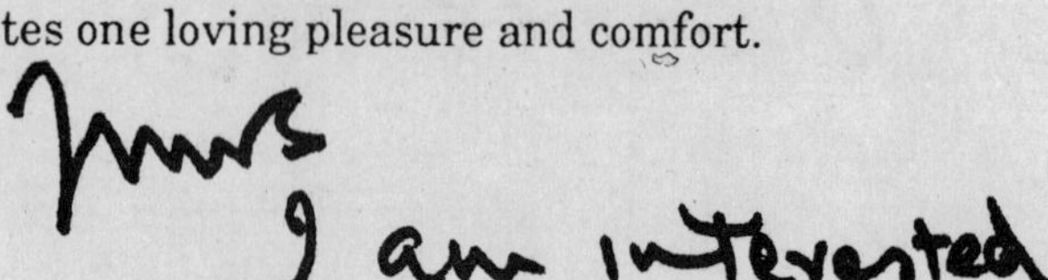

8. Capitals made very plain. Denotes a keen mind.

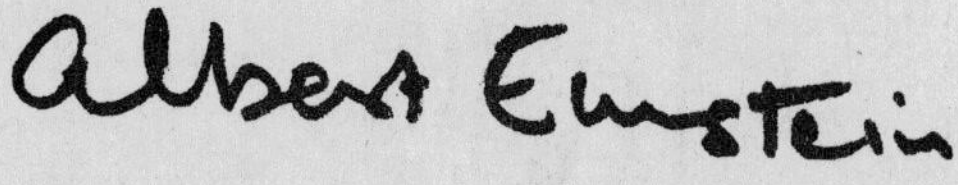

9. Capitals made plain, angular, and awkward looking.

   Denotes a plain, unemotional, tactless nature.

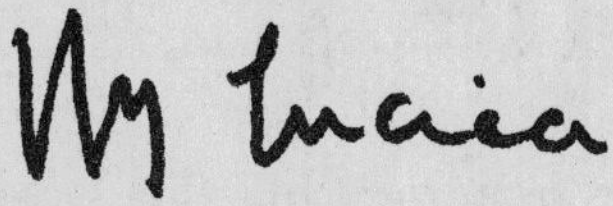

10. Capitals Printed.

    Denotes a person with constructive ability; one with an exacting nature.

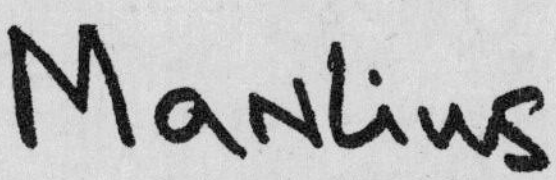

Capital Letter M

1. First stroke of M higher than others,

   Denotes one proud of family name and social position; independent.

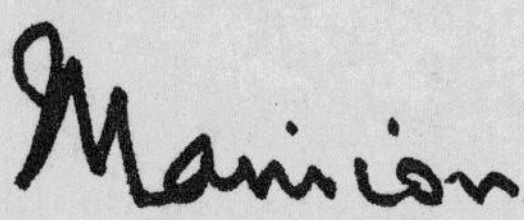

2. Second or third stroke of M highest.

   Denotes a nervous, erratic unreasonable person; hard to get along with; extra imaginative.

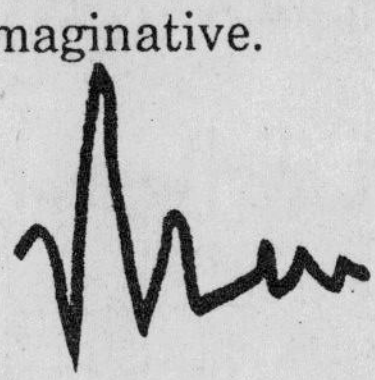

3. M made with three vertical strokes and one horizontal stroke.

   Denotes one who likes nice things; refined tastes.

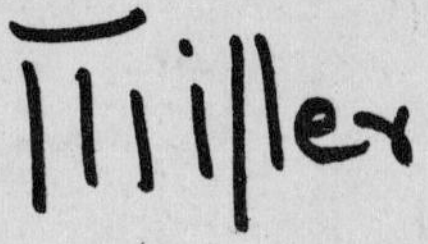

4. M elaborately looped on incurve or at end of third stroke.

   Denotes an ostentatious, uncultured nature.

5. Incurve on M swings from right to left cutting through letter.

   Denotes a sensitive, self appreciative nature. One who is proud and self reliant.

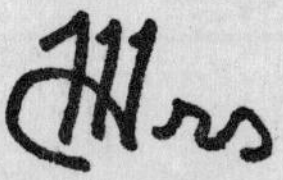

Size

1. Very small writing, so small that it is very hard to read.

   Denotes an extremely introspective person; one not apt to be very communicative or to have any really close friends.

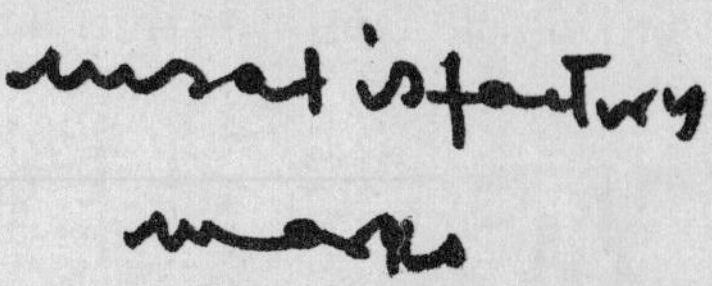

2. Small writing, smaller than one is accustomed to seeing on letters one receives, but not unusually small.

   Denotes a scientific mind.

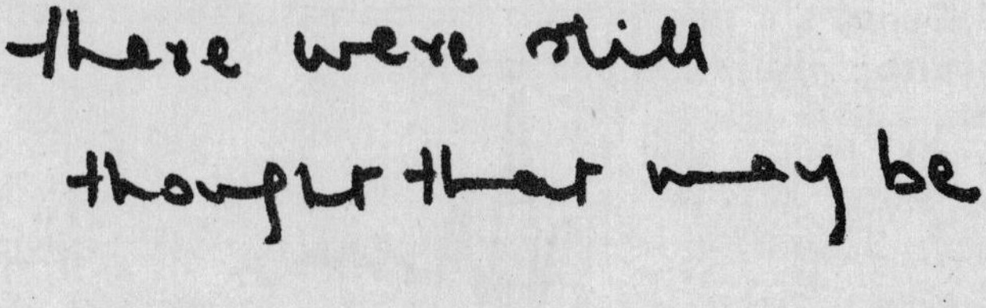

3. Medium sized writing, writing which is the size one sees on most letters one receives.

   Denotes a person with average tastes, ideas, and desires. One easy to get along with and one not apt to expect too much of a person. Practical and materialistic; leaning toward the physical type.

4. Large writing, definitely too large for the sheet on which it appears.

   Denotes an extroverted person, one who is not happy unless he is surrounded by plenty of friends. One who finds it difficult to concentrate, restless nature, can't stay long at one task. Veneer personality, close to surface.

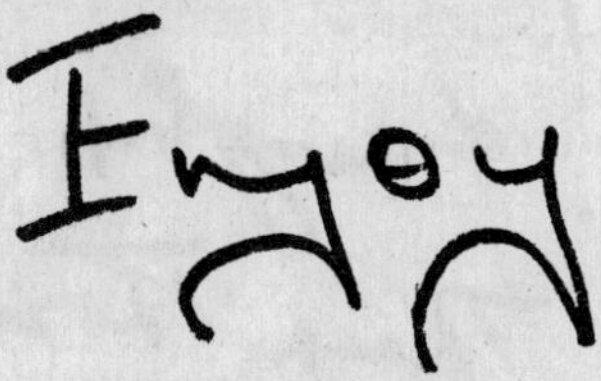

5. Large, flourished writing with deliberate shading.

   Denotes a boasting pompous nature.

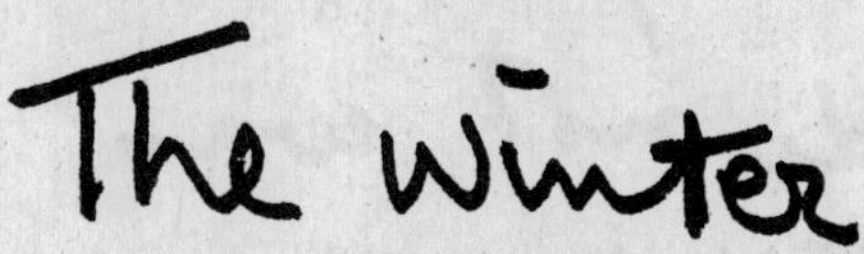

6. Abnormally large and angular writing.

   Denotes one easily excited and possessed with tremendous enthusiasm. Self willed.

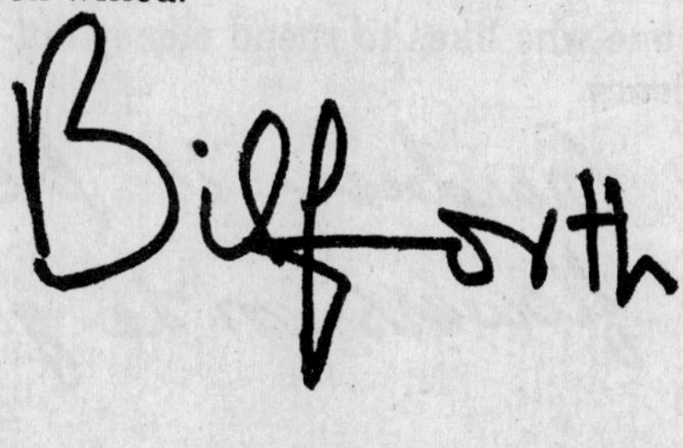

7. Variable in size. Small letters of varying sizes ranging from one sixteenth inch upwards.

   Denotes a childhish, immature nature. One who is the complete servant of his feelings. One apt to be credulous, self centered, and over expressive. Thoughtless of other people's feelings. Indecisive.

Margins

1. Margins wide on both sides.

   Denotes an artistic, aesthetic nature. One who likes harmony and order. Original in ideas. One who would be very fussy over details.

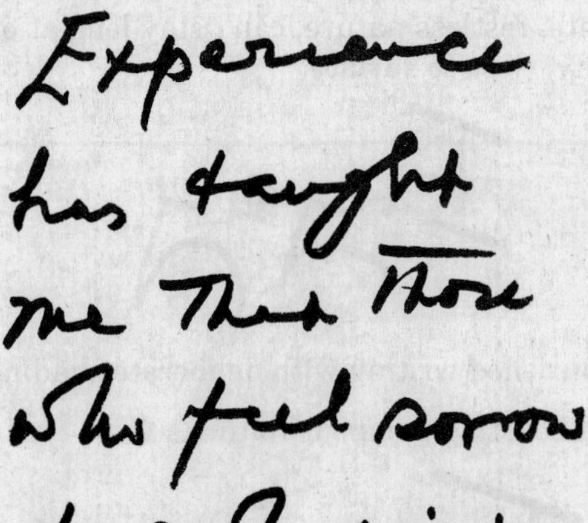

2. Left margin beginning wide and ending narrow.

   Denotes one who likes to spend money but successfully checks this tendency.

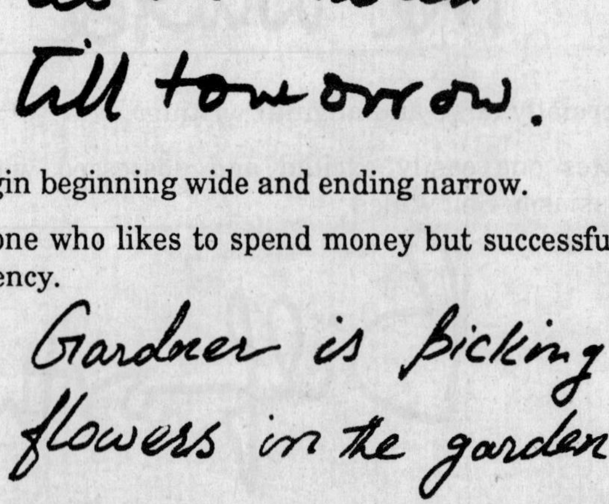

3. Left margin beginning narrow and ending wide.

Denotes one who likes to save but who cannot hold on to his money.

If you love something
set it free. If it
comes back it is
yours. It it does
not it never was.

4. Uneven left margin.

Denotes a lively, careless nature. One lacking in system.

As of today, it seems
that the third World war
will start on the issue
of disarmament!

5. No margins used; all space available for writing made use of.

Denotes a stingy, parsimonious nature. Lacking in good taste and untidy in appearance.

O! You beloved of my
27 senses, I love you,
you, yours, you to you,

Legibility

1. Legible writing.

   Denotes a slow but accurate thinker.

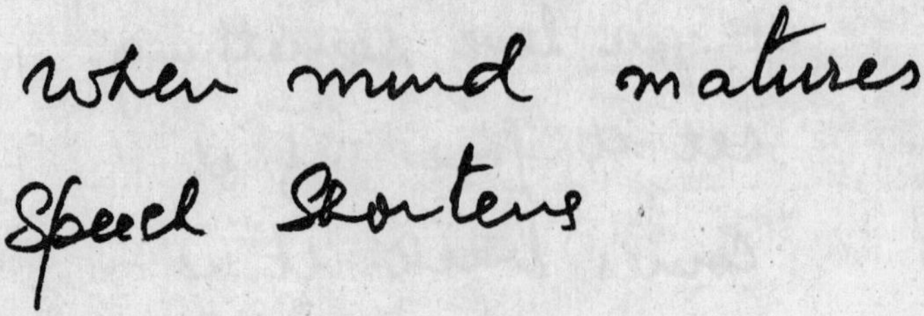

2. Illegible writing.

   Denotes a fast, less accurate thinker. Strong individuality.

   Note: Illegibility is the result of rapid writing wherein the pen tries to keep pace with a speedy flow of thoughts.

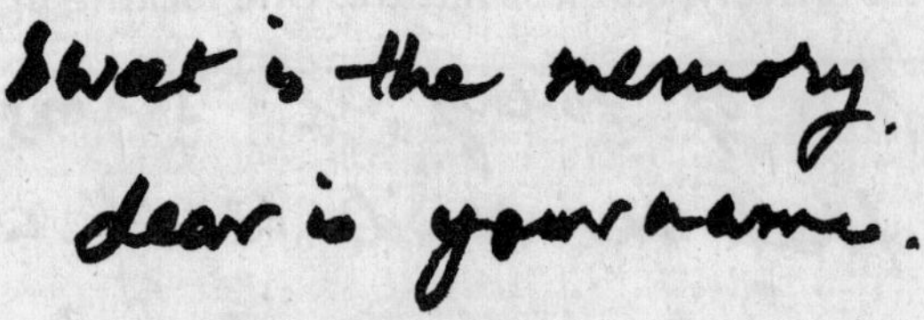

Punctuation

1. Absence of Punctuation. Punctuation is lacking occasionaly Small t's left uncrosed here and there, with an occasional i or j undotted.

   Denotes an absent minded nature. One apt to be late in keeping appointments. One lacking in caution and negligent of details.

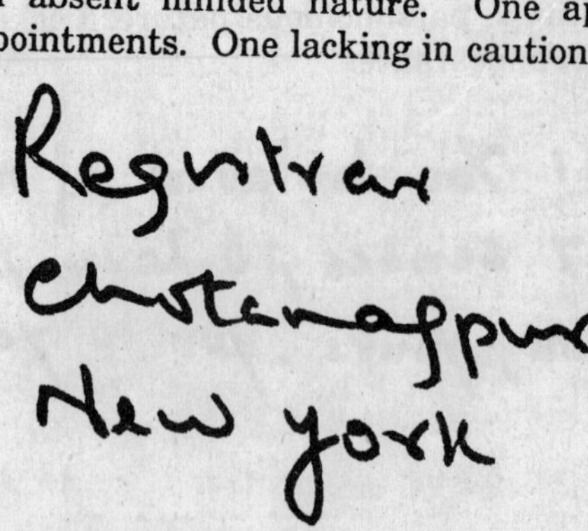

2. Careful punctuation. Small t's crossed with precise stroke and small i and j dotted with even pressured, heavy dots.

   Denotes a person who will hold you to the letter of your agreements with him. One who can be depended upon to function well in an emergency. A very orderly nature.

   Improve - we have stopped all extra curricular activities

3. Careless punctuation. Small t's left uncrossed more than half the time; also, small i left undoted, and commas left out.

   Denotes a thoughtless nature. Apt to be lacking in tact and liable to make many costly mistakes. Not to be depended upon in an emergency.

4. Dashes used in place of periods. Dashes of varying lengths used in place of periods to fill out line of words.

   Denotes practical nature, one not easily fooled. Aggressive.

   music workshop in conducting -

5. Period made quickly resembling elongated dashes.

   Denotes an excitable nature. Never found in a refined hand.

   except my working

6. Periods made round and deliberate.

   Denotes a calm disposition.

   all the religions Christianity

7. Frequent use of exclamation, interrogation, quotation marks, and underscore.

   Denotes one who is romantically inclined. One who becomes easily enthused over things claiming his personal interst.

   Children !! My son of family, here for the !

8. Needless and constant use of quotation marks.

   Denotes an odd nature; one weak in intellect.

9. Accurate use of punctuation, especially colon and semicolon.

   Denotes one with literary ability or training.

   She's interested in music e.g piano

10. Comma habitually left out.

    Denotes a confused mind.

11. Words often underlined.

    Denotes a feeling for accuracy, but also, a tendency to exaggerate.

    Sports

    Dancing

12. Words or phrases set off in parenthesis.

    Denotes a capricious nature; one possessing delicate feelings.

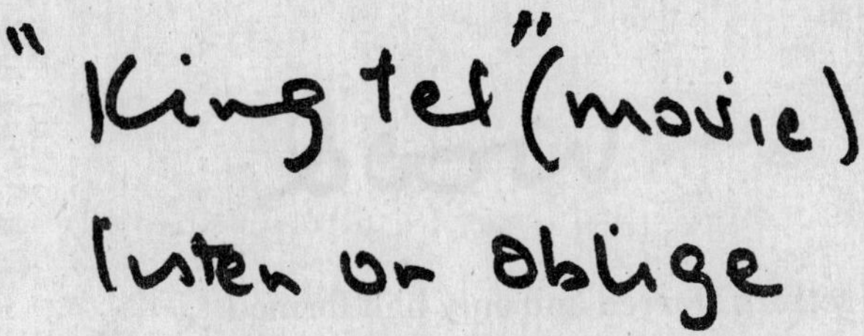

Uniformity

1. Small letters all same size.

   Denotes a consistent person.

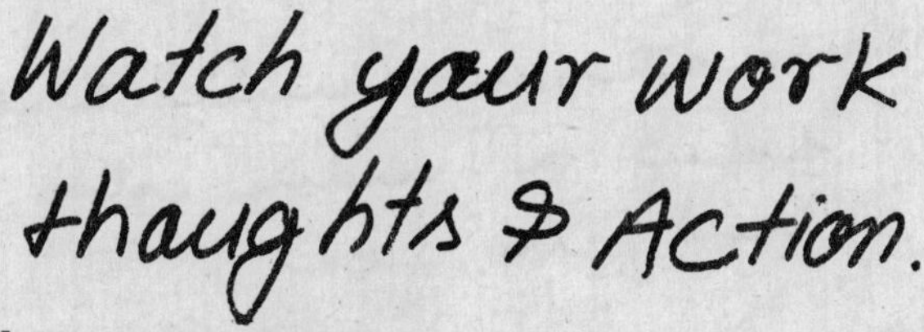

2. Small letters of varying sizes.

   Denotes a person having a taste for change and variety. One not to be depended upon in an emergency.

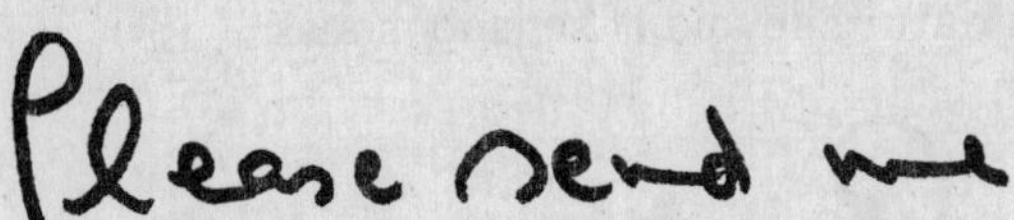

3. Small letters decreasing in size at end of word.

   Denotes a tactful, diplomatic person. One who does not tell you everything that is on his mind.

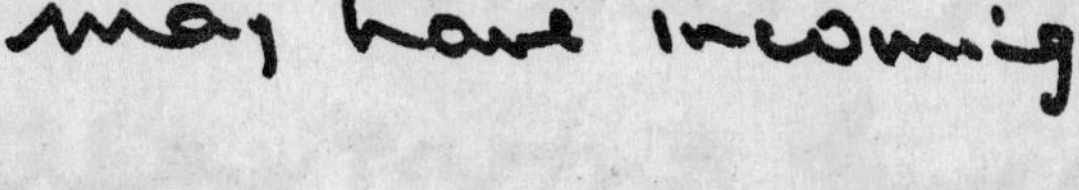

4. Small letters larger at end of word.

Denotes a conscientious nature. One with high personal standards. Honest and straightforward. One easily imposed upon.

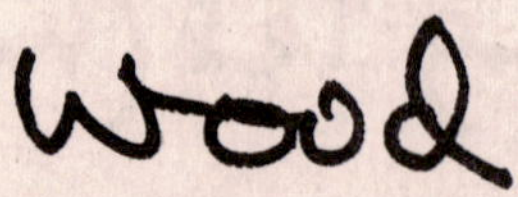

5. Small letters slurred and only half formed.

Denotes one who is impatient with unimportant details; hates fuss and bother. One who likes to get things finished as quickly as possible. An evasive and secretive nature.

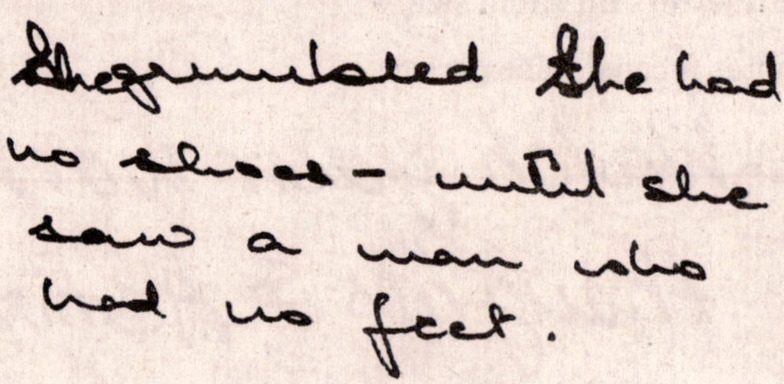

Strokes

1. Cross strokes light; no shading.

Denotes a nature devoid of sensuousness.

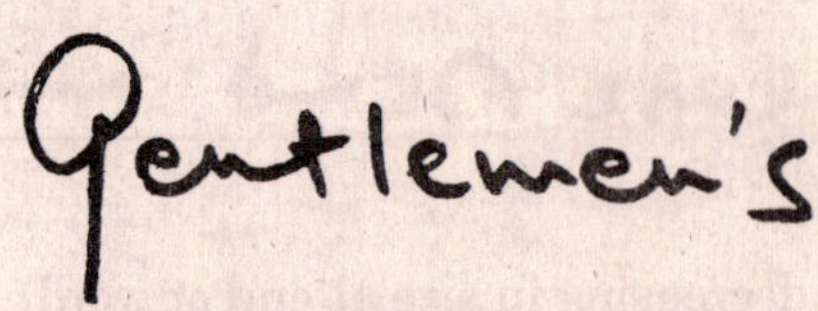

2. Cross strokes heavy and shaded.

Denotes one sensuous to music, art and human emotions.

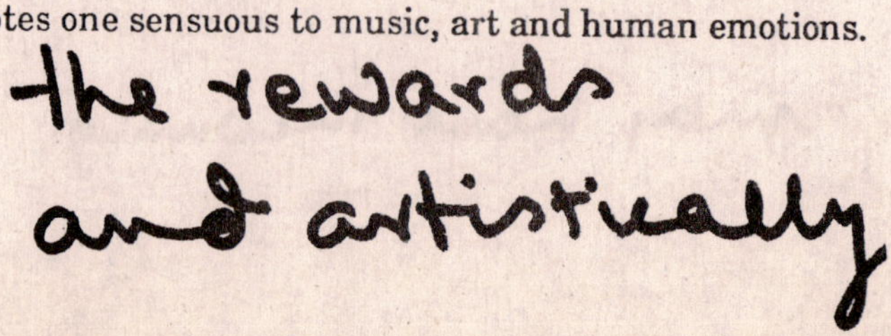

3. Initial stroke absent in letter.

Denotes one patient and self controlled.

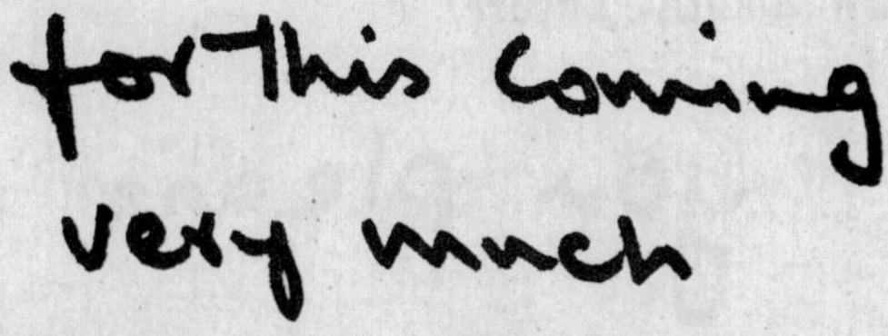

4. Initial stroke tiny.

Denotes one possessing a quick temper.

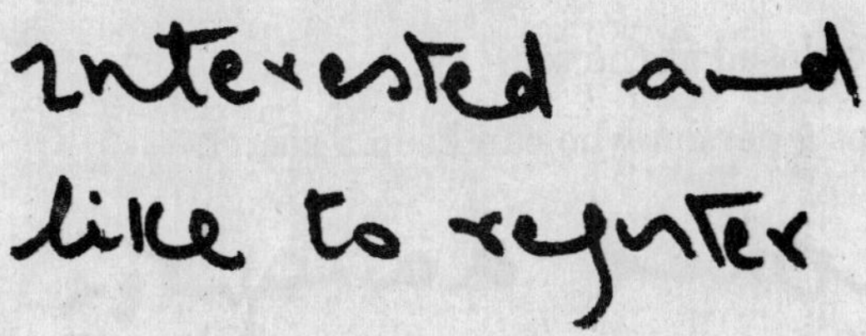

5. Initial stroke a hook.

Denotes one having a possessive, egotistical nature.

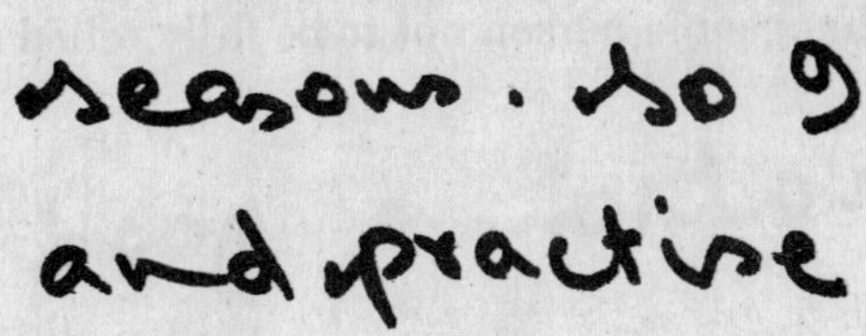

6. Initial stroke curved.

Denotes a person with a sense of humour.

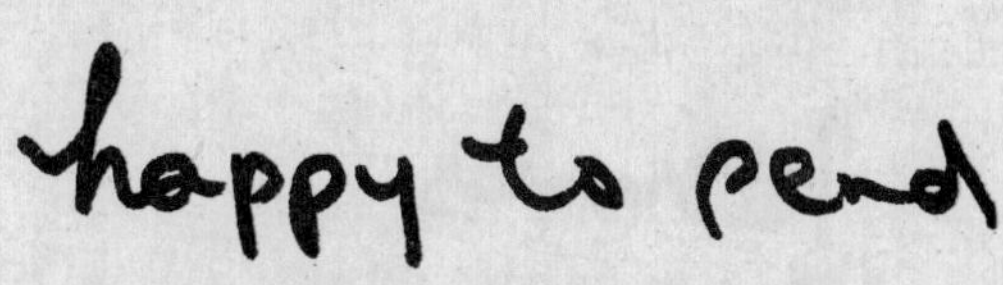

7. Initial stroke long and inflexible.

Denotes a quarrelsome, impatient person.

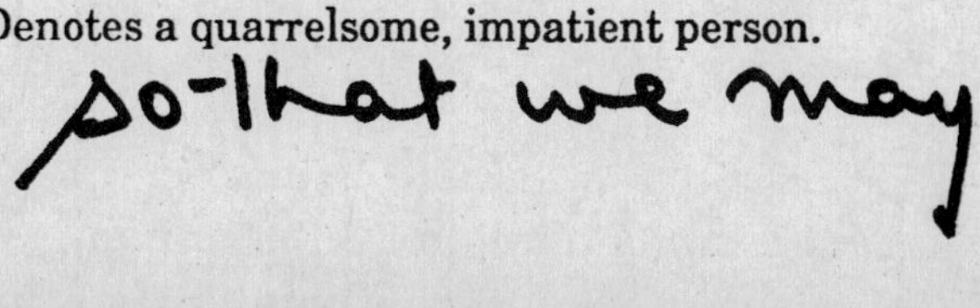

Small Letters (a and o)

1. a and o open at the top.

   Denotes a talkative nature.

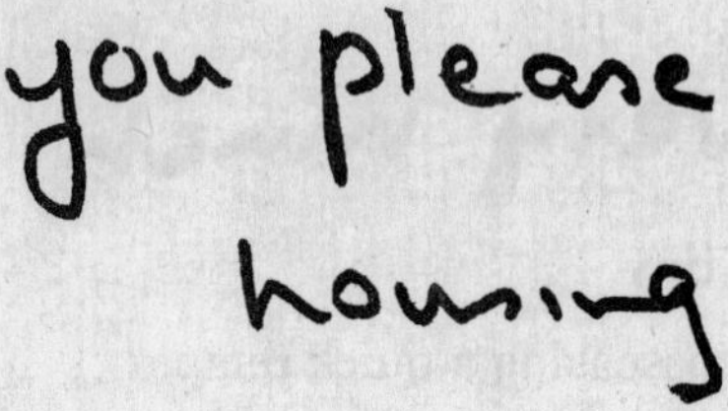

2. a and o closed at the top.

   Denotes a person who can keep a secret.

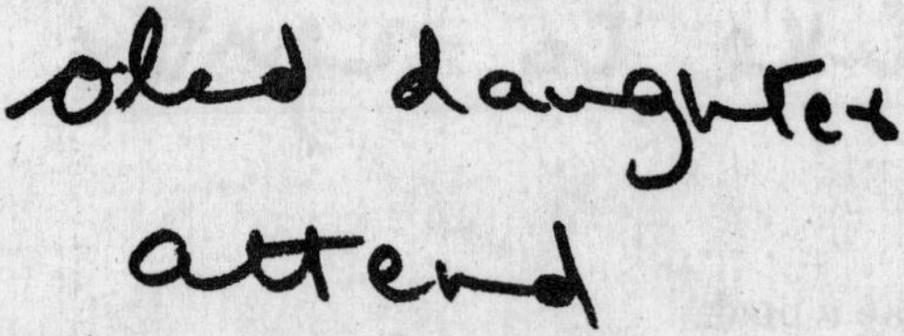

3. Some a's and o's open at top, some closed.

   Denotes a changeable person not to be fully relied upon.

4. a and o knotted at the top.

   Denotes a close mouthed person.

5. a and o open at the base.

   Denotes a dishonest person.

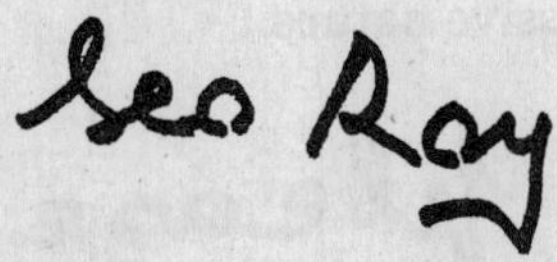

Small Letters (m and n)

1. Small m and n made angular, appearing like w and u.

   Denotes an adaptable nature; one who is good mixer; one with a keen perception.

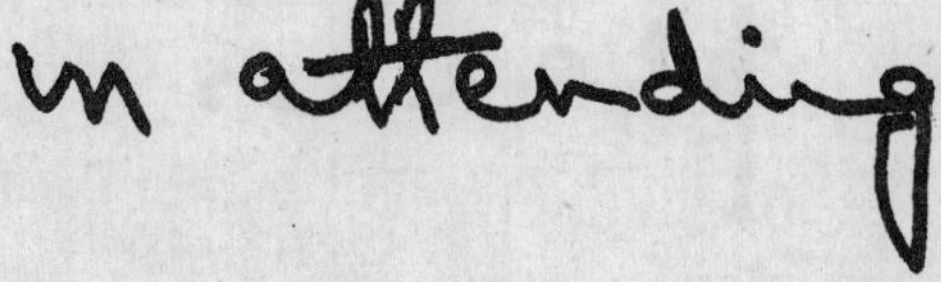

2. Small m and n made rounded, not appearing like w or u.

   Denotes an unadaptable nature; one possessing simple tastes.

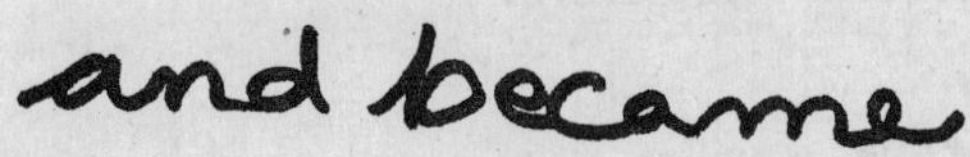

Small Letter (p)

1. Lower loop of small p long with full swing to left.

   Denotes a lover of the outdoors; physical ableness; one who enjoys exercise.

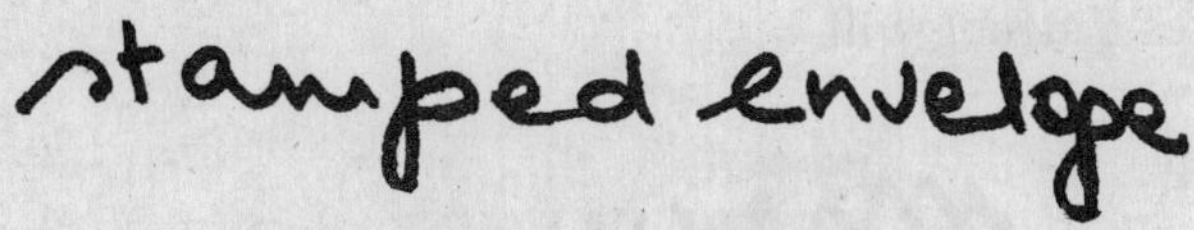

2. Stroke or loop of p made long above and short below.

   Denotes one lacking in physical strength.

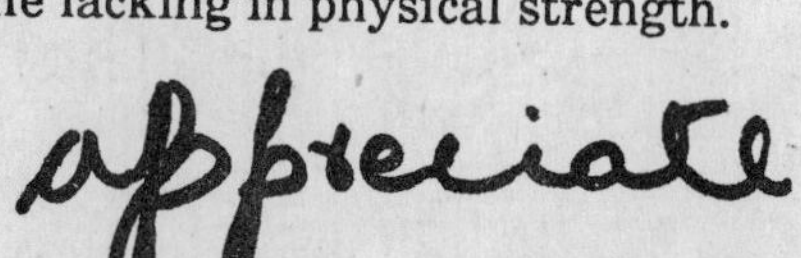

3. Lower point of p sharp with upstroke ascending on right of stem.

Denotes an aggressive nature.

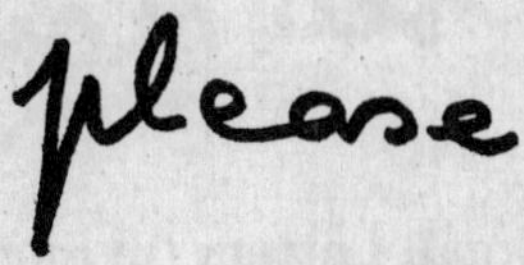

4. Stroke or loop of p made short above and long below.

Denotes one having muscular strength.

5. Lower point of p rounded and ascending upward on left of letter.

Denotes a peace loving nature.

T Bars

1. t-crossing made heavy.

Denotes a strong will.

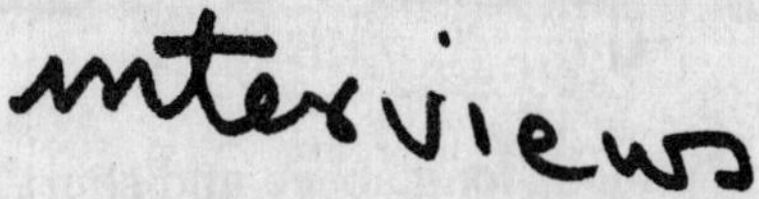

2. t-crossing light and careless.

   Denotes a weak will.

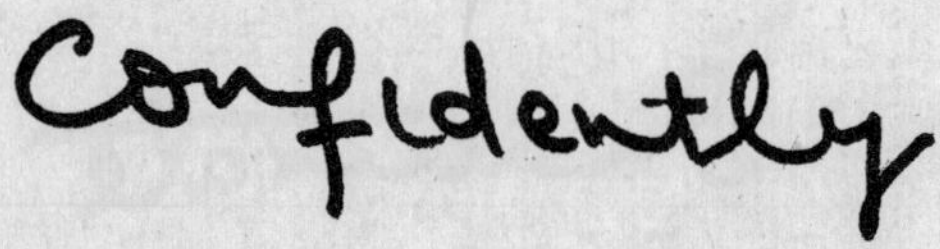

3. t-crossing made wavy.

   Denotes a flirtatious nature.

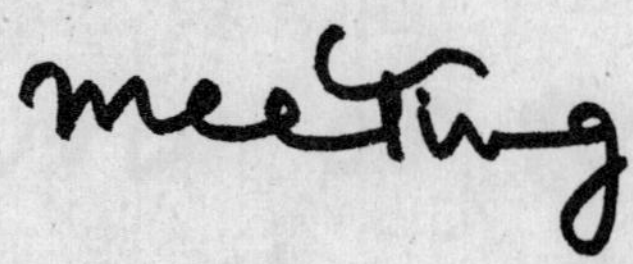

4. t-crossing hooked downward on one end.

   Denotes a determined nature.

5. t-crossing hooked upward on one end.

   Denotes a vindictive nature.

6. t-crossing hooked on both ends.

   Denotes a person with an indomitable will that will seldom admit defeat.

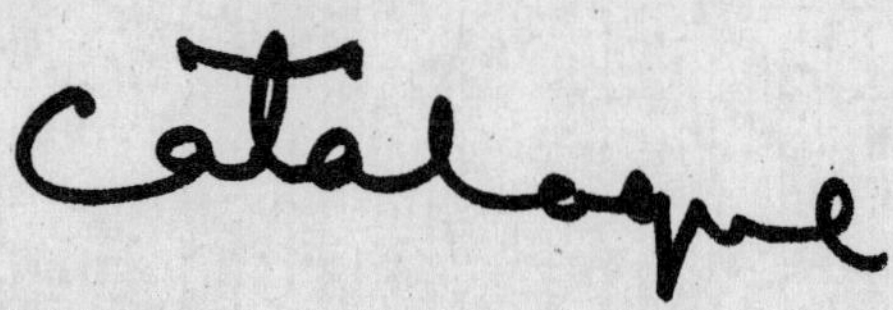

7. t-crossing made very long.

   Denotes an ambitious nature.

8. t-crossing made very short.

   Denotes a repressed nature.

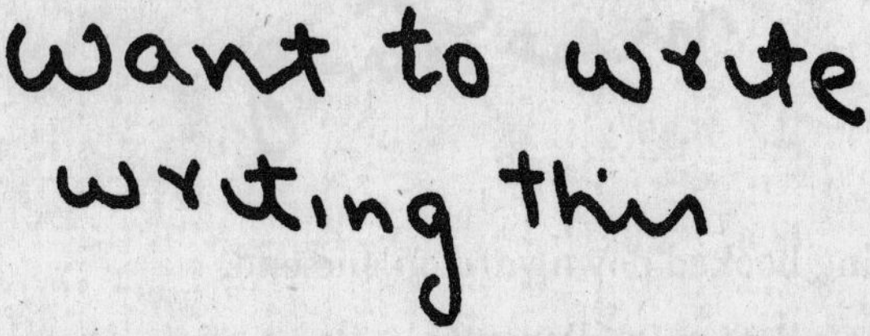

9. t-crossing flourished.

   Denotes a slight eccentricity.

10. t-crossing made to left of stem.

    Denotes a procrastinating nature; and indecisive and weak personality.

11. t-crossing made to right of stem.

Denotes a person full of enthusiasm impulsive.

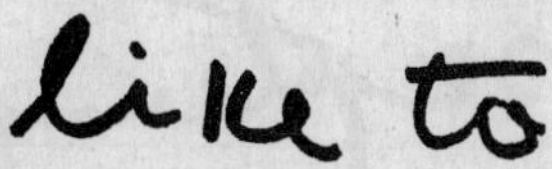

12. t-crossing slanting downward to right.

Denotes a pungnacious, argumentative person; one who will express his opinion whether wanted or not.

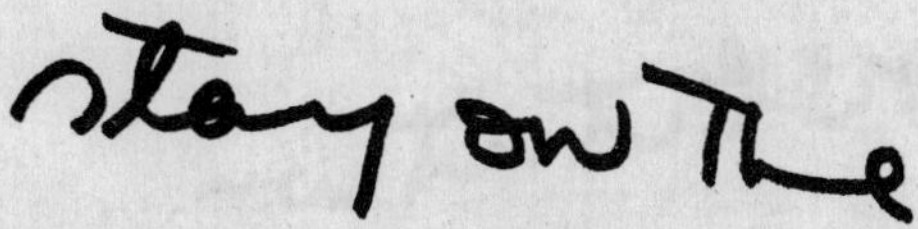

13. t-crossing thick, club-like and slanting downward.

Denotes a brutal coarse nature.

14. t-crossing lance-like.

Denotes a sarcastic, sharp nature.

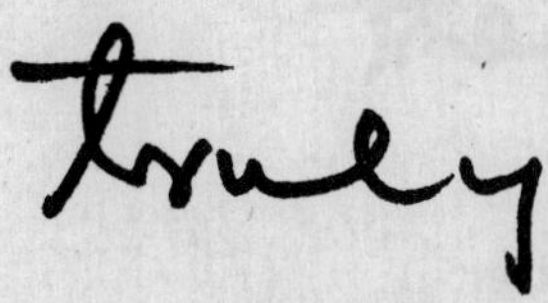

15. t-crossing made with convex curve.

Denotes a self controlled person.

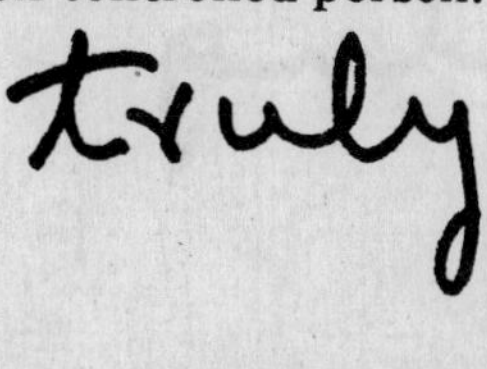

16. t-crossing soaring upward.

Denotes an ambitious, imaginative nature.

17. t-crossing made with concave curve.

Denotes a person easily led to an indulgence in physical appetites.

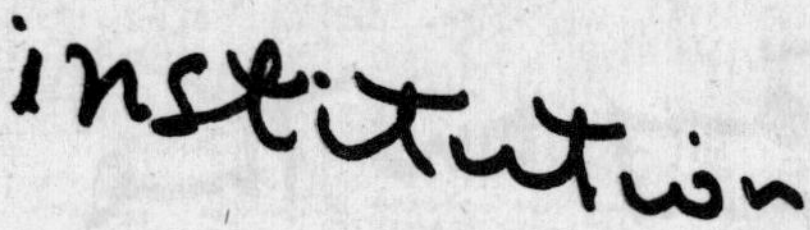

18. t-crossing looped close to stem.

Denotes a persistent nature.

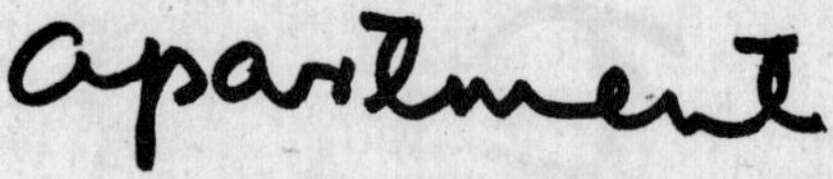

19. t-crossing star shaped.

Denotes a super sensitive nature.

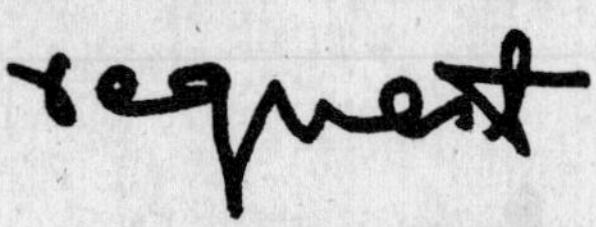

20. t-crossing made above letter.

Denotes an adventurous, imaginative spirit.

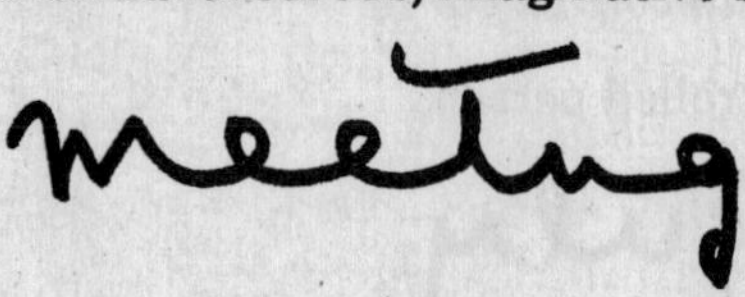

21. t-crossing lacking.

Denotes a lack of self confidence.

22. t-crossing gracefully looped.

Denotes a person with keen sensitiveness.

23. t-crossing made without lifting pen from paper.

Denotes a sensitive nature.

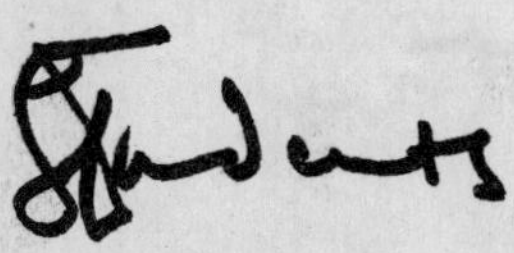

24. Variety of styles of t-crossings.

Denotes a person still in the adjustment stage. He is still trying to find which things should be of most importance to him. His philosophy of life is still in a state of flux.

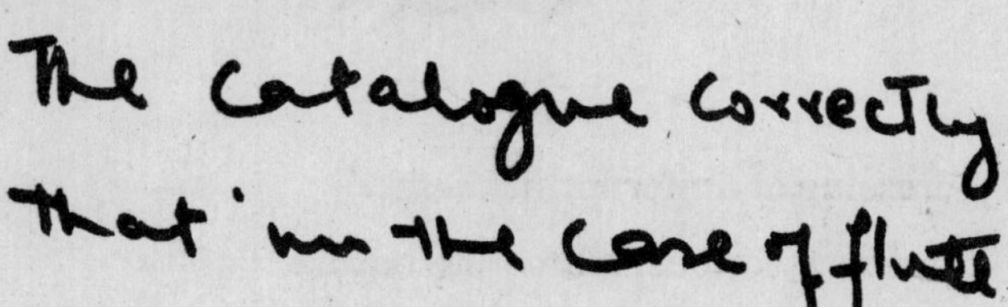

25. t carefully crossed.

Denotes a calm, sure, certain nature.

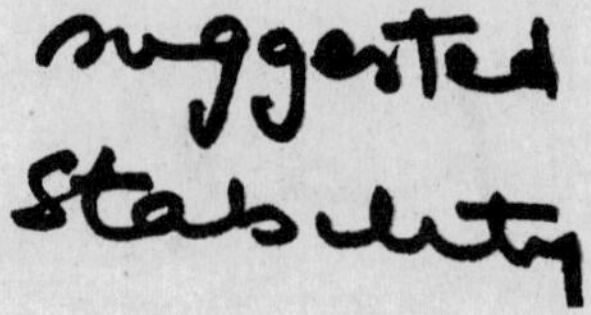

26. t-stem looped.

Denotes a talkative disposition. One who takes offense easily

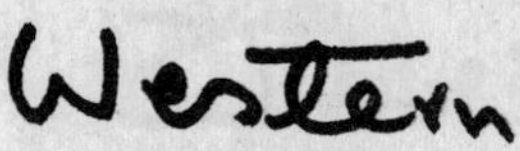

27. t-stem pointed instead of looped.

Denotes a reserved and dignified nature.

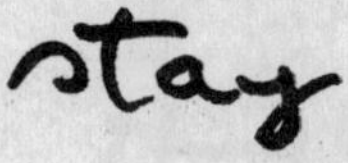

28. t-stem open at bottom; tent shaped.

Denotes a person deceptive and evasive.

29. t-crossing of uniform thickness.

Denotes a serious, temperate nature.

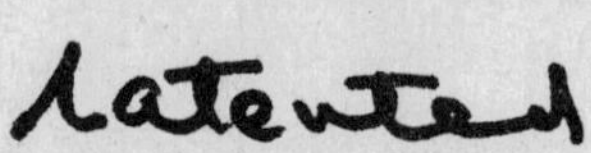

Style

1. Angular. Writing has a jagged, angular appearance.

   Denotes a vibrant, energetic personality. One who gets things done. One not happy unless he is busy doing something.

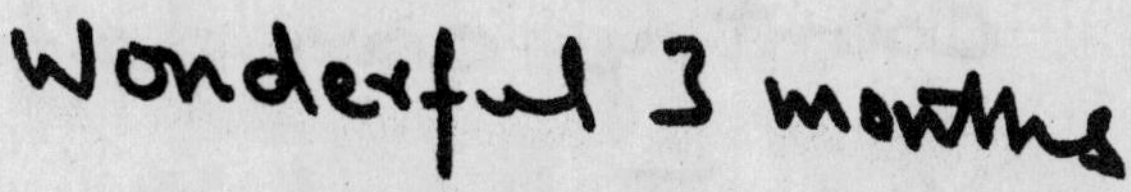

2. Rounded. Writing has a soft, rounded appearance. Small letters have curved tops.

   Denotes a sympathetic nature. One easily imposed upon. One apt to be too credulous for his own good.

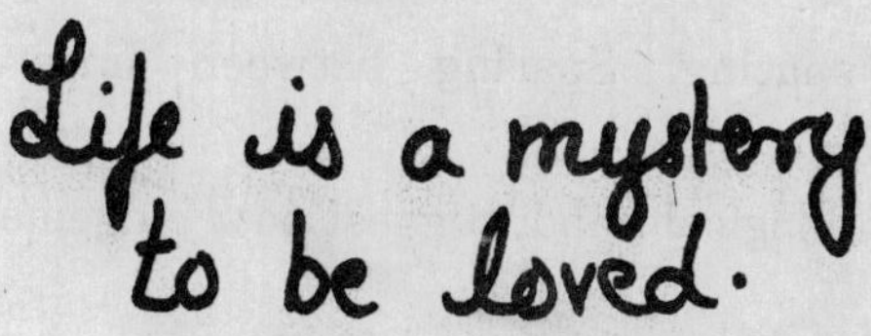

3. Mixed. Combination of angular and rounded writing.

   Denotes a changing personality. Continual conflict between head and heart, selfishness and unselfishness, and between the physical and mental. Unsettled state of mind.

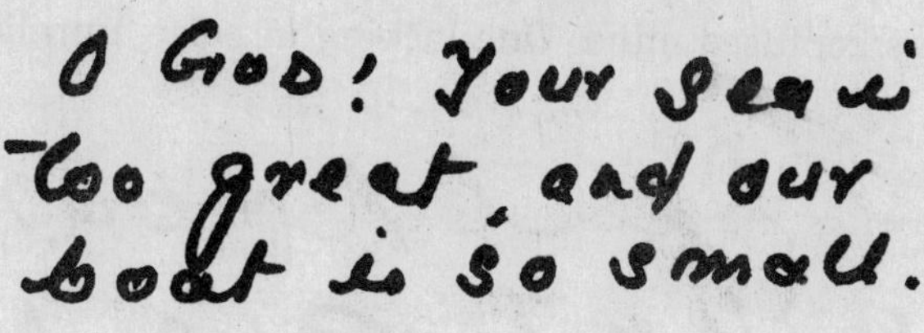

Spacing

1. Regular spacing. Spacing between lines and between words, evan and consistent.

Denotes a logical, well balanced mind; suggests good judgement.

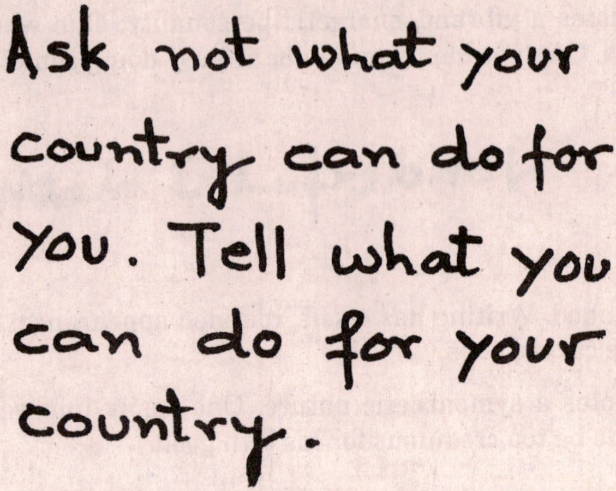

2. Irregular spacing. Spacing between lines irregualr and inconsistent.

   Denotes an illogical mind; suggest poor judgement.

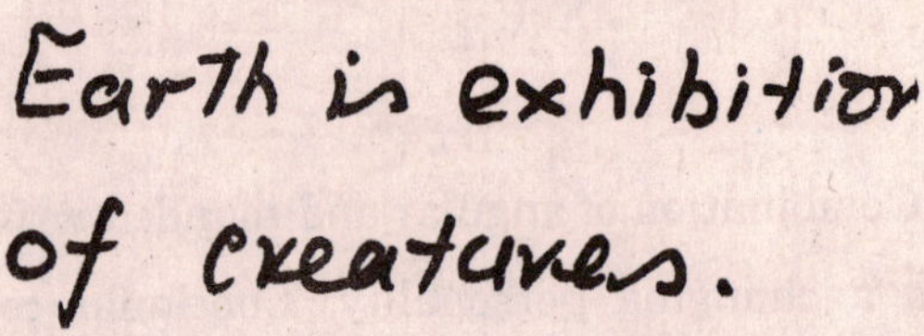

3. Tangled writing. Spacing very irregular with loops of one line running into loops of other lines.

   Denotes a confused mind. One lacking in poise, unreliable and a poor financier.

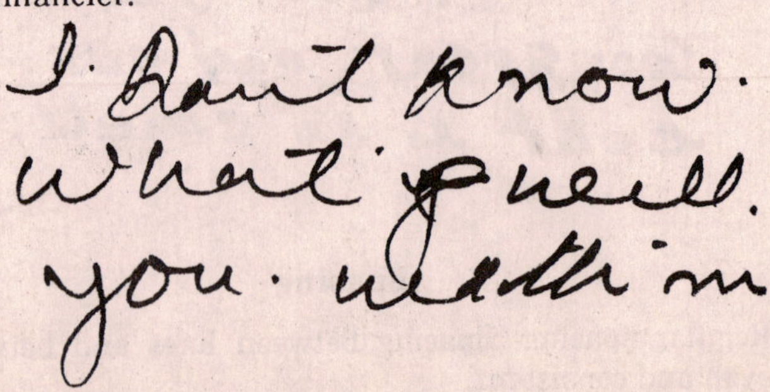

4. Crowded writing. Letters in a word crowded, words also crowded; loops of one line running into loops above and below.

   Denotes one with a narrow mind. One apt to worry too much about little things. Introspective and thoughtful.

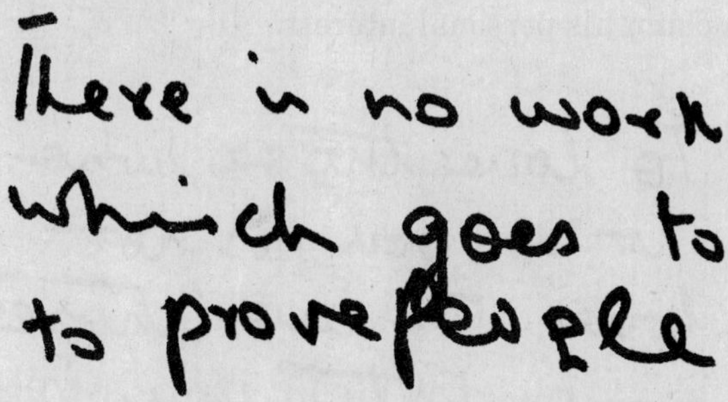

5. Letter compressed. Letters so close to each other that they seem to be lying on each other.

   Denotes one given to economizing and saving; one apt to be avaricious.

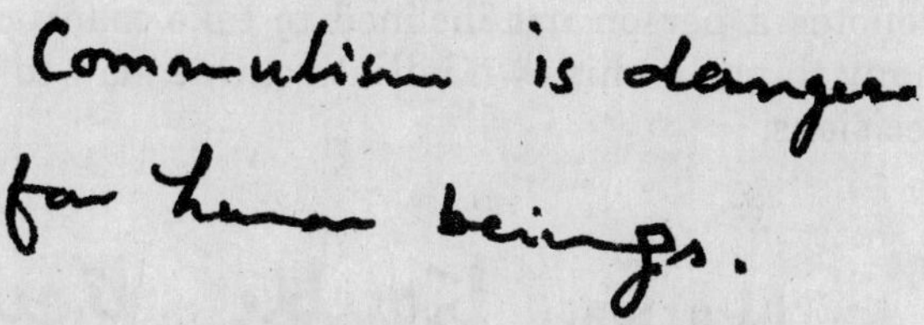

6. Diffused writing. Words and letters spread out unduly.

   Denotes an extravagant nature. One with a superficial nature, hating hard work. Gets things done quickly. Lacks concentrative ability.

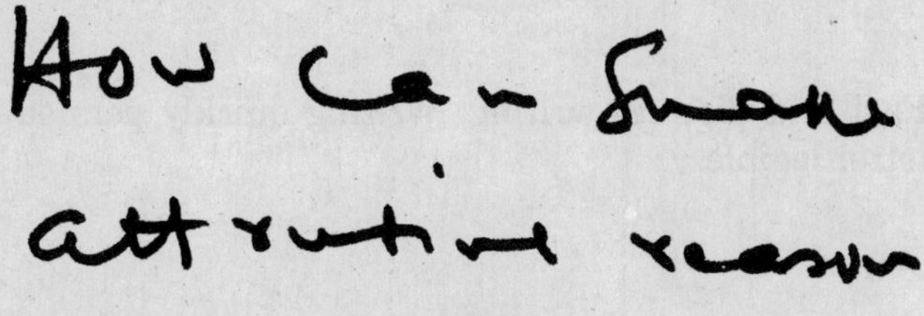

Speed

1. Fast writing. Writing streams along in continuous flow. No interruption in strokes.

   Denotes a person with lots of energy and enthusiasm for things which claim his personal interest.

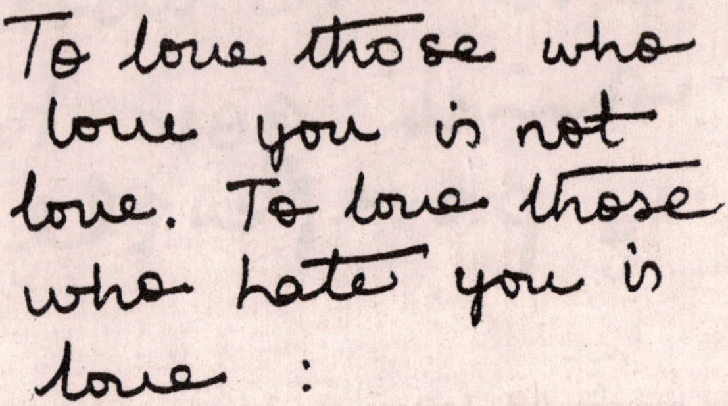

2. Slow writing. Writing is large and strokes are made surely indicating slowness of movement.

   Denotes a person not inclined to take many chances or to do many things on his own initiative. One slow to make important decisions.

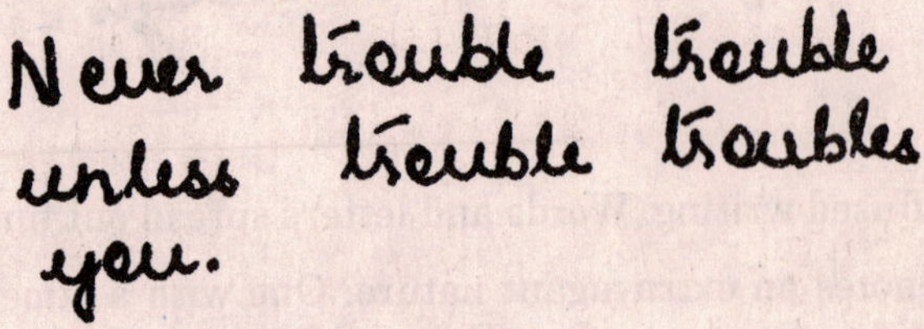

3. Fast and distinct writing. Writing quickly penned with every letter legible.

Denotes one intolerant of details; possessed of a quick, animated nature. One who hates to do things according to prescribed form.

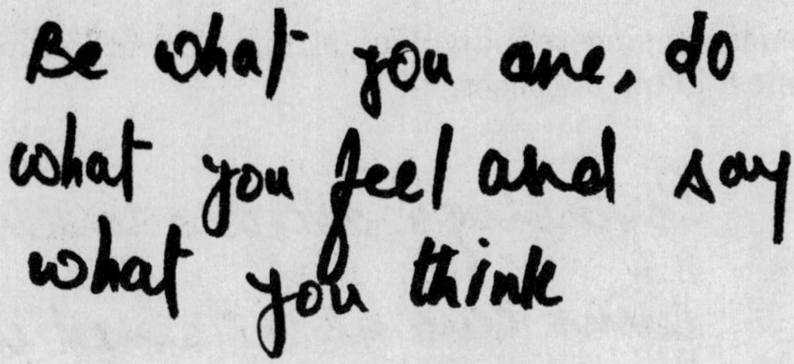

4. Fast and indistinct writing. Some letters only half formed; occasional final letter left out.

   Denotes strong individuality and force of character. Usually talented in some direction. Entertaining taker; ambitious; good imagination.

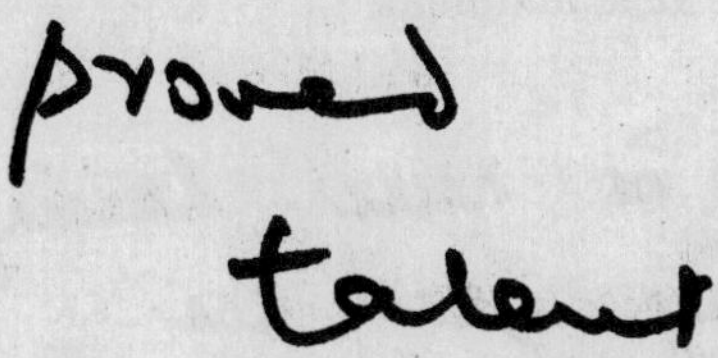

5. Fast writing, dwindling finals, Last few letters dwindle off into stroke.

   Hypocritical unjustworthy nature; scheming and dissimulating self willed.

Lines

1. Straight. Base line of writing is even; a ruler placed along the line of writing will help in determining the straightness of the line.

   Denotes a sincere individual, straightforward in his actions and honest in his purposes.

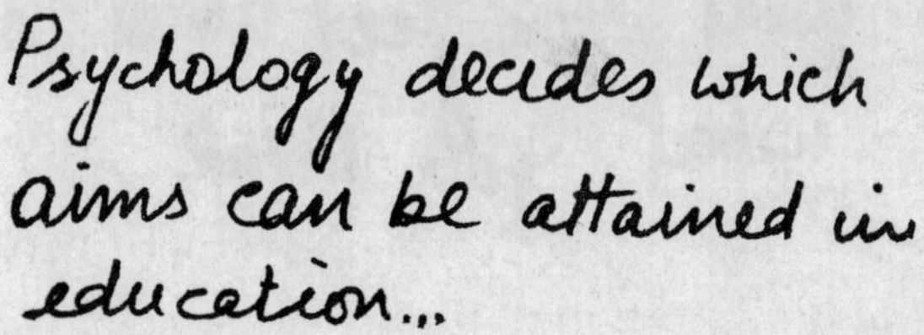

2. Ascending lines. Line of writing tends to rise.

   Denotes a lively, ambitious nature, One not easily discouraged; able to smile in the face of defeat.

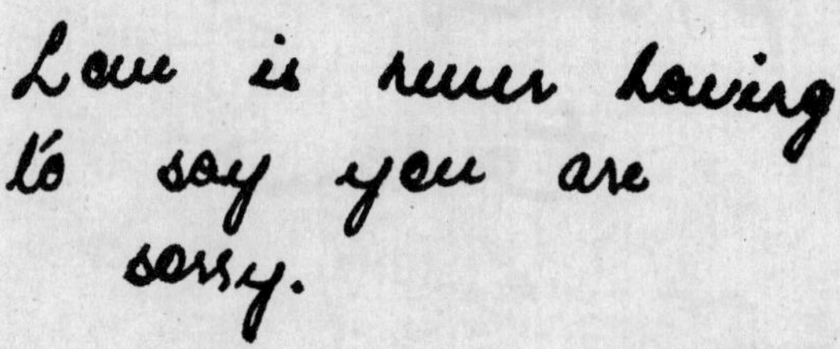

3. Lines ascending then dropping.

   Denotes one with initial enthusiasm which peters out.

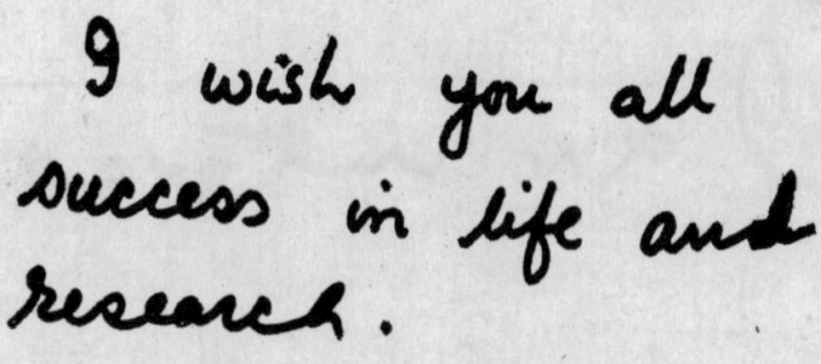

4. Lines ascending to unusual degree.

   Denotes a visionary, over ambitious, impractical nature.

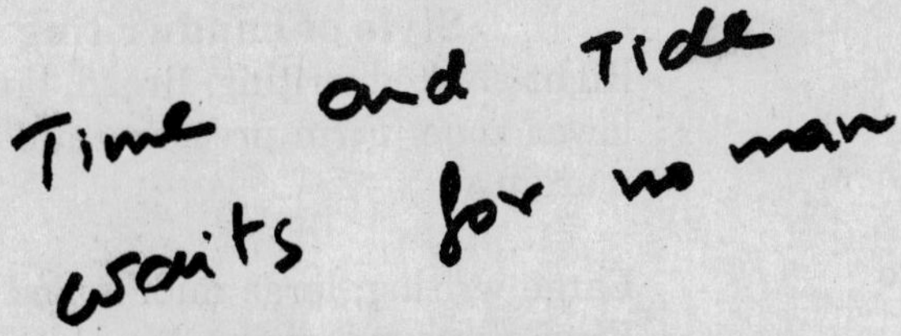

5. Lines descending then rising.

   Denotes one who has difficulty in getting started but once he has begun he finishes his task.

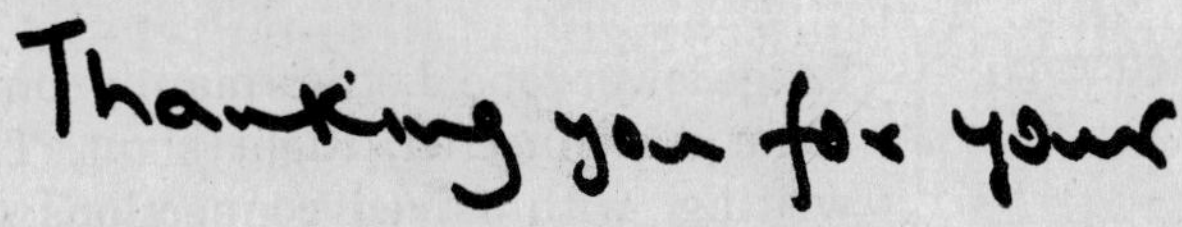

ABC guide to Graphology

Quality	Style of handwriting
Adventerous	Right-slanted writing. Broad, large upper and lower zone. Firm pressure and narrow right margin.
Ambition to Dominate	Large writing, large middle and upper zones. Firm pressure, rising lines, large signature; and strong, rising 't' crosses placed high on the stem.
Amiability	Medium-size writing of average width with fluent, harmonious rhythm, rounded letters and garlands.
Business Sense	Large lower zone. Letters mainly connected but some disconnected. Right slant. Thread-like writing, with mixed connections or angles. Broad, medium or large size. No right margin.
Calm and Poise	Upright or left-slanted regular writing, rounded letter forms, straight lines, regular spacing.
Carelessness	Irregular writing, thread-like, broken letters with the bodies incomplete.
Cold Nature	Left-slanted writing, narrow, sharp stroke. Angular letter connections and words far apart.
Conventionality	Copybook connections. Writing medium size or small. Straight lines, upright or right slant with balanced zones and regular word spacing. Letters connected.
Decisiveness	Angular connections, regular writing, careful letter forms.
Economy	Narrow, small writing with no end strokes to letters. No margins.

Efficiency	Regular writing with angular or copybook connections. Carefully formed letters, with 'i' dots and 't' crosses accurately placed.
Extravagance	Large, broad writing, with wide left margin, large spaces between words and lines.
Extrovert Personality	Large, broad writing with a right slant. Large middle-zone words near together, with all the space filled.
Generosity	Large, broad writing, with large garland end strokes to letters.
Good Judgment	Clear, regular, legible, medium-size writing, letters connected. Upright or slight slant. Straight lines and margins.
Imagination	Large, broad writing. Letters disconnected. Large upper and lower zones with full loops, irregular writing.
Indecision	Thread-like connections, broad, irregular writing with lack of definition in letter forms.
Inferiority Feelings	Small, narrow writing with light pressure and left slant. Descending lines; small personal pronoun I.
Introverted Personality	Small, narrow writing with a left slant. Small middle zone and words far apart with space left vacant.
Modesty	Small writing, small signature, small personal pronoun 'I' and small upper and middle zones to letters.
Obtrusiveness	Very broad writing with firm pressure and angular connections.
Optimism	Rising lines with a dynamic, lively stroke and rounded letter forms. Signature clear and rising, placed to the centre or right.

Pessimism	Falling lines and falling words with angular connections and broken letter forms. Signature crossed through or placed to the left.
Precision	Regular writing, straight lines and margins, Letters clearly and meticulously formed with angular connections. Accurate placing of 'i' dots and 't' crosses.
Secretiveness	Writing completely connected with arcades or copybook, vowels such as 'o' tightly looped and sealed, cover strokes-retracing letters.
Self-Confidence	Large, regular writing with large middle zone. Upright or slight slant. Large signature and large personal pronoun 'I'.
Self-Discipline	Regular writing, straight lines and margines and even word spacing. Balanced zones and upright or slight slant.
Sensuality	Thick, 'pasty' stroke, broad writing but narrow word spacing. Large lower zone to letters.
Sociability	Broad, legible writing with harmonious rhythm. Right slant and words close together. Large middle zone, letter Connected with garlands. Rounded letter forms.
Tact or Diplomacy	Medium or small writing of average width with rounded letter forms and even pressure. Garlands, arcades or mixed connections. Upright or slight slant. Words decreasing in size and wide spaces between words.
Talkativeness	Large, broad writing, connected with garlands. Words and lines close together.
Temper	Right slant with heavy pressure and angular connections. Fierce, pointed or thickened 't' crosses and hooked starting strokes, or starting from well below the base line.

Timidity	Upright or left slant. Narrow, cramped letter forms, light pressure and large right margin.
Unpredictability	Changing slant, irregular writing and varying connections.
Unsociability	Illegible, disconnected writing with a left slant and the words far apart.
Versatility	Irregular writing with some letters connected and others disconnected. Rhythmic, fluid and varying letter forms with threads, garlands or arcades.
Warm Nature	Broad writing with a 'pasty' thick stroke, rounded letter forms and words close together. Right slant.

All The Secrets Of PALMISTRY For Profession And Popularity

Rs. 75

PROF. DAYANAND

• The lines on the palm reveal not only the past and the present, but also the future which lies in store for an individual. The Institute of Palmistry seeks to enlighten you on this subject.

• The book is the result of more than 30 years of experience of the subject by the Chief Instructor of the Institute of Palmistry Prof. Dayanand. It reveals the secrets of the lines on your hand and other signs which have not been revealed in any other book published on the subject so far.

• The subject has been explained with the help of hundreds of illustrations. You can learn to read a hand once you have gone through this book. You can use the knowledge either to earn money or for popularity among your friends and relatives.

* HOW TO BE HAPPY, HEALTHY & RICH

S.N. BOSE

Rs.40

* A MEANINGFUL LIFE

M.P. LAKHANI

Rs. 40

DISEASES: CURED BY YOGA

100% safe way to perfect health

- Asthma (Damaa)
- Obesity (Motaapa)
- Diabetes (Madhumeh)
- Tuberculosis (T.B.) (Tapedik)
- Piles, Fissure, Fistula (Bawaseer, Bhagandar, Nasur)
- Improving Height
- Blood Pressure Heart Diseases
- Rheumatic Arthritis (Jodon ka Dard)
- Indigestion (Badhasm)
- Backache (Peeth ka Dard) and Spondylitis
- Urinary & Seminal Diseases (Mootra Aur Virya Vikaar) and Hernia
- Constipation (Kabz)
- Sweat Control (Paseena Niyantran)
- Flatulence (Pet Ki Gais)
- Skin Diseases (Charam Rog)
- Worms (Pet Ke Keede)
- Navel and Jaundice (Naabhi Aur Peeliya)
- Women Dieases
- Hair
- Throat Diseases
- Eyes
- Concentration (Ekaagrata)
- Common Cold, Cough and Catarrh (Zukaam, Khaansi Aur Nazla)

RS. 8/- EACH

HEALTH SERIES:

TRADITIONAL FAMILY MEDICINE

- Harad and Baheda (The Terminalies)
- Gourds and Pumpkins- The Family Cucurbitaceae
- Amalaka and Bhumi Amalaka
- Onion and Garlic
- Neem and its Relatives
- The Banyan and the Peepul
- Khas, Kesar, Nagakesar, Khaskhas
- Coconut, Supari, Kikar and Catha
- Bael, Wood Apple, Lemons, Castor
- Ginger and Turmeric
- Salt, Sugar, Jaggery and Honey
- Spices of India
- Isabgol, Gokhru and Brahmi
- Seasoning Herbs of India
- Some Fragrant Herbs - Tulasi and the like
- Milk and Milk Products
- The Greens
- Some Common Vegetables of India
- Some Indian Fruits
- Karkatashringi, Indubar, Nauvasadar and Fitkari

Rs. 25/- each

Post free (in India) if full money sent in advance

D K P D (P) Ltd

1, Ansari Road, Darya Ganj, N. Delhi-110002. Ph: 3261465, 3278368

Biographical Sketch of MAHABHARAT Characters	**Great Epics of India : PURANA**
• Bhagwan Sri Krishna • Veda Vyas • Bheeshma Pitamaha • Dronacharya • Daanveer Karna • Dharamraj Yudhishthir • Bhimasen • Veer Arjun • Nakul • Sahadev • Duryodhan • Shakuni • Gandhari • Kunti • Draupadi • Shantanu • King Pandu and Dhritrashtra • Drupad, Virat and Shalya • Abhimanyu, Jayadrath, Ghatotakach and Ashwatthama • Vishwamitra, Parshuram and Vasishtha • Vidur & Sanjay • Who's Who of The Mahabharat	• Brahma Purana • Padma Purana • Vishnu Purana • Shiva Purana • Bhagavata Purana • Narada Purana • Markandeya Purana • Agni Purana • Bhavishya Purana • Brahmavaivarta Purana • Linga Purana • Varaha Purana • Skanda Purana • Vamana Purana • Kurma Purana • Matsya Purana • Garuda Purana • Brahmanda Purana • Vayu Purana
Rs. 20 each	**Rs. 20 each**